SOURCE OF THE LIGHT

SOURCE OF THE LIGHT

A Witness and Testimony of Jesus Christ, the Savior and Redeemer of All

MAURINE JENSEN PROCTOR
SCOT FACER PROCTOR

Designed by Kent Ware

Deseret Book Company
Salt Lake City, Utah

Library of Congress Cataloging-in-Publication Data

Proctor, Maurine Jensen.
    Source of the light : a witness and testimony of Jesus Christ, the
Savior and Redeemer of all / Maurine Jensen Proctor, Scot Facer
Proctor.
       p. cm.
    Includes bibliographical references.
    ISBN 0-87579-648-6 (trade). — ISBN 0-87579-666-4 (gift)
    1. Jesus Christ—Mormon interpretations—Pictorial works.
2. Palestine—Antiquities—Pictorial works. 3. Palestine—
Description and travel—Views. I. Proctor, Scot Facer, 1956–
II. Title.
BX8643.J4P76 1992   92-27973
225.9'1'0222—dc20   CIP

ISBN 0-87579-648-6 (trade edition)
ISBN 0-87579-666-4 (limited edition)

Printed in Mexico

10 9 8 7 6 5 4 3 2 1

CONTENTS

PERSONAL NOTES

Page 6

1 I AM HE WHO WAS PREPARED
FROM THE FOUNDATION
OF THE WORLD

Page 10

2 BEHOLD THE
LAMB OF GOD

Page 40

3 THAT THEY MIGHT HAVE
LIFE MORE ABUNDANTLY

Page 82

4 MINE HOUR
HAS COME

Page 136

5 THEN SHALL THEY KNOW
THAT I AM THE LORD

Page 184

NOTES

Page 206

PERSONAL NOTES

Photographs, in and of themselves, never tell the full story. You won't see the stray cat that walked through the doorway in our nighttime exposure of a Jerusalem home. The exposure took eight minutes, and even the cat's hesitation in the doorway wasn't long enough to show up on the film. You won't see the crowds that cluster at every site significant in the life of Christ. We waited, sometimes for hours, nervously watching light conditions change, until that brief minute when no one was in the scene. You won't see the blue barrel in the distance at Tel Be'er Sheba. Our daughter hefted it behind a rock and then hid herself so she wouldn't show up in the picture.

To capture the Savior's life in photographs, however, is to find out how deeply Israel bears record of Him. The land is His visual aid, the echo of everything He said, with meanings lodged in every tree and stone. We once thought His message was completely devoid of the time and place He gave it. As we shot pictures in olive vineyards and sheepfolds, as we watched for sunrises on the Galilee, we found that His message is in the land itself. In every way, Bethlehem was designed by nature and history to be His birthplace. The anguishing atonement should have been suffered in a place with olive trees and a press. We hope you'll come to learn why on this photographic journey to the lands of the Savior.

A visit to Israel shatters one's old and sometimes cherished ideas about the place. Whoever wrote "Far, Far Away on Judea's Plains" had simply never been there. Israel is not flat and brown but mountainous, and in the springtime its hills are brushed with a colorful palette of flowers. We shot the pictures for this book in Israel's wettest year in recorded history, and even the stark Judean wilderness was touched with green. Christ's birth was not on a frosty, snow-covered night, the baby laid in a wooden manger. The sounds of springtime accompanied His birth, and the manger was probably stone, the Middle-Eastern feeding trough for animals.

Shooting the photographs for this book was no small task, as we entered the Middle East with an eighty-seven-pound camera bag, a large tripod, 350 rolls of film, eleven suitcases, and two of our daughters. Through all of our travels and flights, we boldly protected our film from X-ray machines at least fifty-five times (including the flights into the Arabian Peninsula), saying things to guards who spoke only Hebrew or Arabic: "Film very, very sensitive," or "Is very special film." Sometimes it would take thirty minutes just to talk our way through security in broken explanations and foreign tongues.

We went to Israel with a schedule, hoping to shoot certain sites on certain days, but a few days into the trip we tossed our schedule and decided to follow the light, intently watching the sky and listening to the Spirit. Many days we were up at two or three in the morning, traversing dangerous roads to set up our equipment in pre-scouted locations and wait. Offering all of our skills, the best equipment, the finest film, our

Above: Close to the summit of one of the mountains above the valley of Dothan in northern Samaria. Near this place the servant of Elisha was told, as Israel's enemies encompassed them, "Fear not: for they that be with us are more than they that be with them. . . . And the Lord opened the eyes of the young man, and he saw: and, behold, the mountain was full of horses and chariots of fire round about Elisha."[1]

Left: Carpet of flowers touched by the precious gift of rain near the road to Jericho. Seldom seen in such abundance in the Judean desert, these vibrant colors bespeak Isaiah's prophecy that as the righteous gather to Israel, "the wilderness and the solitary place shall be glad for them; and the desert shall rejoice, and blossom as the rose."[2]

greatest plans—all was nothing unless the Lord painted the picture for us. It was a deep lesson for us to see "that it is by grace that we are saved, after all we can do."[3]

One dark and overcast morning, we left our kibbutz and traveled ninety minutes to the banks of the Jordan River, expecting to arrive just before sunrise. It was one of those days photographers dread—hazy, gray, diffused. We drove down a dirt road to the location we had found the day before. The tripod was locked, the shutter set, the depth of field marker aligned, film waiting. Nothing. We couldn't even tell if the sun had risen. We knelt down in the dirt by the tripod and pleaded with the Lord to paint a picture that would testify of His Son's baptism. We ended our prayer, and seconds later clouds broke, the beams of light began to pierce the heavens, and we fired away. When we were done, the sky returned to itself, hazy, overcast. We prayed over every picture and saw daily miracles.

Hoping to capture the scene as it might have appeared nearly two thousand years ago, we shot Bethlehem at dawn on April 6, the true birth date of the Savior. We went to the Kidron Valley and shot Absalom's Tomb on the very night, based on the Jewish calendar, that Jesus would have walked from the Last Supper through the Kidron past that tomb and on to Gethsemane. The moon was nearly full, casting shadows through the olive vineyards, and we almost felt that if we could just disappear into the shadows and be quiet enough, we could see the Lord and His apostles walk by. It was on a night like this, we thought, a night just like this.

Often, the scenes we saw were teaching moments for us. The waters of the Sea of Galilee were slate gray the morning we waited for the fishermen to arrive. We had come at dawn to shoot a picture of fish. The foreign tongues of the merchants who had gathered were mainly Hebrew and Arabic, but the rabbis spoke Yiddish, which we could understand. "The first three boats are coming," they said. Finally we could see dots on the horizon and then distinguishable shapes moving in toward the small harbor. We quickly got the big Pentax ready, bulky tripod and all. The crowd gathered to see the fish for which they would bargain for their restaurants and markets. The two men on the first boat looked bone-weary and haggard. They had toiled all night to bring in a catch. One burly man, his face lined with exhaustion and goodwill, asked in Hebrew what we were doing there. The rabbis explained briefly that we needed a picture of some fish. He turned to us and in broken English said, "If you want picture of fishermen, you can have. If you want picture of fish, you cannot; we have none." We could see that ancient scene in our minds as seven of the apostles came toward shore in the morning with empty nets after fishing all night. Unrecognizable to them, the resurrected Savior stood on the shore and asked, "Children, have ye any meat?"[4] Then He told them to cast their nets on the other side, and they pulled in a multitude of great fishes. When they saw the abundance, they knew immediately it was the Lord who had given.

We have felt the Lord's gifts and know that what He promises, He is able also to perform. Our journey to the Sinai desert in a rental car was delayed until later in the afternoon than we had hoped to leave Cairo. Nevertheless, we drove swiftly toward the Suez Canal, calculating an arrival at the holy mountain about 8:30 that evening. The darkness gathered to pitch by the time we turned east, following the map. All was going well as we raced into the darkness on schedule, knowing that a 2:00 A.M. start up the mountain would be needed to catch first light and sunrise. Up ahead it looked like we were coming upon a very steep descent. We slowed down to nearly thirty miles an hour, and suddenly the road ended—without sign or warning. The car literally flew a number of yards as we went off the pavement, dropping three feet to the dirt and rocks below. With hearts pounding and ears perked for adverse noises from the Fiat engine, we inched our way forward on this now four-wheel-drive road. Construction was taking place, but there were no indications of any kind as to how to detour around the repairs. Flashing our lights, we discovered another dirt road going off to the right. Another mile, now to the left. Now two roads going opposite directions and boulders across the highway in repair.

Unable to even trace our way back, we were lost in the darkness with no food and little water in this stark, ancient, desolate region of the earth. We stopped the car and began to pray, pleading, "Dear Father, please hear us. We are lost and afraid. Please show us the way." Within a minute, out of nowhere, a Toyota pickup full of Bedouins was ahead of us. We had not seen another car all night. Somehow they sensed our need and began to turn on their blinkers and flash their lights to signal to us every turn, every rock, every danger. This went on for nearly two hours, through turns and roads that we could not have followed in the day without a guide. Finally they pulled over, apparently coming to the turnoff to their isolated home. A man in white native dress came over to our car and said in broken English, "Straight, no go left, no go right. Very bad, three kilometers. Then okay to Mount Sinai." His directions were perfect; we arrived safely

but worn thin at nearly midnight. We learned again that the Lord is aware of each of us and sees to our most intimate needs.

We are so grateful for Truman and Ann Madsen of the Jerusalem Center for Near Eastern Studies. Their daily rallying of love, support, and stories was one of the highlights of our experience in the Holy Land. Truman's seasoned suggestions were a wonderful influence on our thinking as we created this book, which we desire to go to all the world. To our precious parents, Paul and Martha Proctor and Maurine Jensen, we are indebted for mortality and bonded for eternity. To our beloved friends, John and Diane Madsen, we are eternally grateful—their thoughts and prayers are felt daily. To Ron Millett, Sheri Dew, Kent Ware, and Jack Lyon of Deseret Book we are so thankful. Sheri is remarkable in her visionary approach to projects, and she has carried us long and far. Kent has become one of our best friends, a man whom we love dearly and thank for the art direction throughout. To Nina and Darrell Ownby we are grateful; they have ever been a support and a strength to us in our lives. We are indebted to Christopher Bigley for his timely help in our home. And to our children we are tenderly thankful. How many thousands of knocks on the door of our home office we have had to turn away to complete the project. Their names need not go unmentioned: Melissa, Laura, Eliot, Julie, Lucas, Rachel, Andrew, Thomas, Truman, and Mariah.

Our hearts are full as we offer this book as our witness and testimony of the Lord Jesus Christ, to whom we look for all things. His atoning sacrifice is the center of our lives. From that witness we desired to do this work, and we give this book to Him, with eternal love and gratitude.

1

I AM HE WHO WAS PREPARED FROM THE FOUNDATION OF THE WORLD

A baby cried in the stillness of a spring night in Bethlehem, and the world would never be the same. Here in the vulnerability and tenderness of an infant was the Lord Himself. Jesus Christ had come to walk the dusty roads of mortality, to know hunger, pain, and rejection—all to ease our burdens. When we kneel at the very limits of our earthly endurance, we can always know that He has been there before us. Yet the story does not begin here. It begins in a time beyond our memory, before our birth, before the veil of forgetfulness dropped over our spirits. There in the premortal world, we all lived as spirit sons and daughters of Heavenly Parents. Called Jehovah, Jesus Christ was the firstborn, the preeminent One of all the sons and daughters of God. John testifies, "In the beginning was the Word, and the Word was with God, and the Word was God. . . . And the Word was made flesh, and dwelt among us."[1] In mortality Jesus prayed, "Glorify thou me with . . . the glory which I had with thee before the world was."[2]

Pages 10–11: Looking north from summit of Jebel Musa, Mt. Sinai, as first light touches ancient, twisted red granite of the holy mountain. From the 7,497-foot peak in the southern region of the Sinai Desert, range upon range of mountains can be seen. Near this place Moses conversed with the God of Israel, "face to face, as a man speaketh unto his friend."[3]

Left: Springs at Dan in northern Israel bubbling forth with clear, cold water from aquifers fed by the snowfields of 9,232-foot Mt. Hermon—source of the Jordan River. The word Jordan means "coming down from Dan."

Above: Red poppies in Galilee, a vibrant reminder of the blood shed in the Savior's sacrifice. The poet writes: "Our birth is but a sleep and a forgetting; The soul that rises with us, our life's star Hath had elsewhere its setting And cometh from afar; Not in entire forgetfulness, And not in utter nakedness, But trailing clouds of glory do we come From God, who is our home."[4]

Above: Sunset over Yam ha-Melah (the Dead Sea) in the wilderness of Judea as viewed from Jordan. In the unbearable heat of summer in this lowest place on earth (1,303 feet below sea level) over 5 million tons of water evaporate from the sea each day. No life survives in this water with 30 percent salt, yet the Prophet Joseph Smith said that the waters of the Dead Sea must be healed before the Son of Man will make His appearance.[5]

Right: Vault of heaven above the mountains of Naphtali in Lebanon overlooking Kiryat Shmona at dusk. "The elements are eternal,"[6] the scriptures teach, and "the word create *[as used in Genesis] came from the word* baurau *which does not mean to create out of nothing; it means to organize; the same as a man would organize materials and build a ship ."[7]*

In that premortal world, a grand council was held, whose results led the morning stars to sing together and all the sons of God to shout for joy.[8] God the Father presented a plan that would enable all of His sons and daughters to progress to be like Him. For each spirit, the plan would involve risk, a leaving home to dwell on earth, a testing. Yet it would also mean the obtaining of a body, an opportunity to prove faithful, a school. "We will go down," the Lord said, "for there is space there, and we will take of these materials, and we will make an earth whereon these may dwell; and we will prove them herewith, to see if they will do all things whatsoever the Lord their God shall command them."[9]

In this world, mortals would, by their very nature, be subject to sin and heartrending weakness. Forgetting everything before that first breath of mortal life, they would err, stumble, sin. Because it is an eternal law that "no unclean thing can dwell with God,"[10] they could not return to their Heavenly Father without a Redeemer, someone who would take upon Himself their sins, making their garments "pure and spotless" again before God,[11] giving new life. It was God's beloved Son, Jehovah, who volunteered Himself as the sacrifice, to take upon Himself all the sins of the world. This would demand a perfect life, a complete submission, a never bending to temptation, an "infinite and eternal sacrifice."[12] "Father, thy will be done," said Jehovah, who would be Jesus Christ, "and the glory be thine forever."[13] I will perform this weighty task, He was saying, not for acclaim or honor, not to upset thy throne, but for love.

We, as sons and daughters of God, must have looked to Jehovah with such trust, knowing that He would not fail us. Without Him we would be forever shut out from our Father; with Him we could have eternal life. "There shall be no other name given nor any other way nor means whereby salvation can come unto the children of men, only in and through the name of Christ."[14] This was the "plan," a term completely missing from scripture until modern revelation. For erring souls on the earth, Jesus Christ would plead our cause: "Father, spare these . . . that believe on my name, that they may come unto me and have everlasting life."[15]

In that premortal council, gifted and cunning Lucifer, called a "son of the morning,"[16] presented his own plan: "Behold, here am I, send me, I will be thy son, and I will redeem all mankind, that one soul shall not be lost, and surely I will do it; wherefore give me thine honor."[17] Lucifer devised an apparently risk-free plan, but one he surely knew would thwart the children of God. He would allow no freedom of choice, no agency. Forced into conformity to law, mortals would not progress or learn, unempowered to choose right or wrong, light or dark. In halting the progress of others, his evil design was to usurp the very throne of God. Isaiah recorded, "Thou [O Lucifer] hast said in thine heart, I will ascend into heaven, I will exalt my throne above the stars of God, . . . I will ascend above the heights of the clouds; I will be like the most High."[18] The desire to dominate, to be first, to crush others is a pattern and inclination that continues to come from this ancient source. Lucifer, who is Satan, swayed many of the hosts of heaven with his flattery, lies, and deception. "Wherefore, because that Satan rebelled against me," said the Lord, "and sought to destroy the agency of man, . . . and also, that I should give unto him mine own power, . . . I caused that he should be cast down."[19]

"And there was war in heaven." At stake was the precious gift of agency and more, the very opportunity for the sons and daughters of God to eventually have eternal life, His life. "Michael and his angels fought against the dragon; and the dragon fought and his angels, and prevailed not; neither was there place found any more in heaven. And the great dragon was cast out, that old serpent, called the Devil, . . . he was cast out into the earth, and his angels were cast out with him."[20] Yet the war in heaven was only the first contest in a struggle that would relentlessly continue, for where were Satan and his minions cast? Onto the earth, where the forces of light and darkness would continue to clash.

The lot of Satan and his followers was to never be given bodies, to never live again in the presence of the Father. In their miserable condition they would strive to lead the children of men astray, cause them to suffer as they suffer, and bring enmity and division into the hearts of people everywhere.

Looking west from the ancient city of Samaria (modern Sabastiya) into the land that was occupied by the tribes of Ephraim and Manasseh in the northern kingdom. For nearly three thousand years the country of Samaria has been divided against Judah. After three years of besieging by Shalmaneser of Assyria, this area was overthrown (in 721 B.C.), and the Ten Tribes were carried away captive and lost to history.

The desert gives forth its glory when water comes to the region. Flowers in a small ravine between Arad and the Dead Sea bursting forth for a few days. The solitary places of the Holy Land seemed to attract the prophets of old—perhaps because in these desolate regions one comes to understand that without God, man is nothing.

B efore I formed thee in the belly, I knew thee; and before thou camest forth out of the womb I sanctified thee, and I ordained thee a prophet unto the nations,"[21] the Lord told Jeremiah, speaking of that time before time, before the foundations of the earth. So it was that the Lord's leaders were chosen and foreordained for the missions they were to perform on the earth. Michael, the mighty archangel who had led the forces of heaven in the war with Satan, "reached great distinction and power before he ever came to this earth: and . . . helped to frame this earth while he was yet a spirit."[22] He became Adam, the first man on earth. "And our glorious Mother Eve with many of her faithful daughters"[23] were among those called to "carry the message of redemption unto all."[24]

Others of the "great and mighty ones"[25] were selected to lead dispensations, those periods of the earth's history when the knowledge, keys, and power of the gospel of Jesus Christ would be given from the heavens. Enoch was chosen to be a leader as were Abraham, Moses, and John the Baptist. Abraham, shown in vision the intelligences that were organized before the world was, said, "Among all these there were many of the noble and great ones; and God saw these souls that they were good, and he stood in the midst of them, and he said: These I will make my rulers; . . . and he said unto me: Abraham, thou art one of them; thou wast chosen before thou wast born."[26]

How were these chosen? "According to the foreknowledge of God, on account of their exceeding faith and good works . . . they . . . are called with a holy calling . . . to teach his commandments unto the children of men."[27] They were not chosen to receive the honors of men or the praise of the world, to impress with flashing, glittering power. Instead, they were selected to serve and to lift, to love, and to carry the gospel of Jesus Christ to the ends of the earth. Their rewards in this life might include deprivation, tribulation, distress and persecution,[28] and they might be stoned or beheaded or crucified. All this was "that the trial of [their] faith, being much more precious than of gold that perisheth, though it be tried with fire, might be found unto praise and honour and glory at the appearing of Jesus Christ."[29]

Shadows of evening begin to steal across the northern portion of the Wilderness of Zin in the Negev Desert with the mountains of Edom in the background. In this region the children of Israel were encamped and very thirsty when Moses smote the rock and "the water came out abundantly, and the congregation drank, and their beasts also."[30] The Lord always tries to teach His children that prophets are His representatives on the earth, and that whether His message is "by [His] own voice or by the voice of [His] servants, it is the same."[31]

Each stream that slides over smooth stones, each eagle that mounts on the wind, each dolphin that leaps in the air was created by Jesus Christ under the direction of His Father. "All things were made by him," John declares, "and without him was not any thing made that was made."[32] Life in its boundless varieties, nature with so many colors in a single wheat stalk that an artist could never paint it, this was the creation that sprang from the heart and soul of Jesus Christ. As creator, He knows every particle, every element, every atom. "For the earth is full," He declares boldly, "and there is enough and to spare; yea, I prepared all things."[33] He is the architect, the designer, the poet, the composer of nature's sweet song, and as each phase was completed He stopped long enough to declare that it was good.

He "laid the foundations of the earth," and "laid the measures thereof," and "stretched the line upon it."[34] He is "in the sun, and the light of the sun, and the power thereof by which it was made. . . . He is in the moon . . . as also the light of the stars . . . and the earth."[35]

As the poem is a reflection of the poet, so the earth in all its bounty and generosity reflects the Lord. "All things are created and made to bear record of me,"[36] says the Savior. The patterns of sleeping and waking, of night being broken by the dawn of a new day, remind us of the resurrection. Daily meals remind us that we are nourished by the sacrifice of death. The spin of the atom and the spin of the earth remind us that the very essence of the universe is built on opposition in all things. As we can read them, even the lights in the heavens are for signs and seasons to teach us about the Lord.[37] The wise men looked upward to see that He was born.

Why this creation with its reminders of the mission of the Lord built into its very structure? The Lord answers clearly, "Behold, this is my work and my glory—to bring to pass the immortality and eternal life of man."[38] To the voice of the Creator, even the dust of the earth will instantly respond; it is only His children who hesitate.

21

Eden. The very name connotes all that is paradisiacal. It was a garden where fruit and flowers came forth spontaneously with colors so exquisite and tastes so sweet as to delight the soul. It was where two people lived in such harmony and unity with the earth that all nature responded with peace. There Adam and Eve, the first man and woman on earth, received the breath of life and instructions from the Father, with whom they walked and talked. "Of every tree of the garden thou mayest freely eat; but of the tree of the knowledge of good and evil, thou shalt not eat, . . . nevertheless, thou mayest choose for thyself, for it is given unto thee; but, remember that I forbid it, for in the day that thou eatest thereof thou shalt surely die."[42]

In this garden, Adam and Eve lived in perfect oneness and companionship. She was his helpmeet, meaning in Hebrew, "a power or strength equal to." Adam calls her "bone of my bones, and flesh of my flesh."[43] "*Bone* in Hebrew symbolizes power, and *flesh* weakness. [This phrase] thus becomes a ritual pledge to be bound in the best of circumstances (power) as well as the worst (weakness).[44]

When first placed in the garden, Adam and Eve had immortal bodies, enlivened by the spirit instead of blood. In this physical condition, they could not die but lived in a state of perpetual innocence. "Be fruitful, and multiply, and replenish the earth,"[45] the Lord said to them, but this presented a dilemma. With these bodies, they could not bear children.

Now entered into this peaceful scene Lucifer as a serpent, hoping to thwart God's purposes. "He sought also to beguile Eve, for he knew not the mind of God, wherefore he sought to destroy the world." He enticed her to eat of the tree of the knowledge of good and evil. When she responded that God had said that in the day they ate, they would surely die, Satan had a ready answer: "Ye shall not surely die; for God doth know that in the day ye eat thereof, then your eyes shall be opened, and ye shall be as gods, knowing good and evil."[46] Satan's tactic was a mingling of deception and truth.

How long Eve considered the decision we do not know. Should she take such initiative in the search for knowledge? Should she pay the price entailed to replenish the earth and bear

children? Here, indeed, was the test of agency, for she could not have it both ways. At last, with some misconceptions and a good deal of courage, she ate, and Adam soon followed. A very real physical change came upon them, with blood coursing through their veins, and their bodies became mortal and subject to disease and decay. For their transgression, they were cast from Eden and the presence of the Lord, entering a world of sin and corruption.

The law had been broken, and the consequences had to be faced. "Cursed shall be the ground for thy sake," the Lord said. "By the sweat of thy face shalt thou eat bread, until thou shalt return unto the ground—for thou shalt surely die."[47] Only through repentance and the atonement of Jesus Christ could they return to the Lord. Eve revealed, "Were it not for our transgression we never should have had seed, and never should have known good and evil, and the joy of our redemption."[48] The pattern was set, and the human family began.

Adam and Eve were cast into a world not as pleasant as the Garden of Eden, for now the earth would yield noxious weeds and tares that would afflict and torment them. Yet Eve did labor together with Adam, and they offered sacrifices unto the Lord, even the firstlings of their flocks. They were instructed by an angel that the sacrifices were "a similitude of the sacrifice of the Only Begotten of the Father, which is full of grace and truth."[49]

Fertile fields and rolling hills of the promised land given by the Lord to Abraham just north of Be'er Sheba. The Atonement of Jesus Christ would apply to the faithful who were born before Him, "that thereby whosoever should believe that Christ should come, the same might receive remission of their sins, and rejoice with exceedingly great joy, even as though he had already come among them."[50]

Cast out from the garden, Adam and Eve were not left to wander in their new world of thorns and thistles in ignorance. From the beginning, they were taught the gospel of Jesus Christ. The gospel was not a new invention during Jesus' mortal life, nor are scholars right who suppose that when they find fragments of the gospel taught before Christ's mortal life, that He borrowed from an earlier source. The gospel of Jesus Christ is of the most ancient origin. "In that day the Holy Ghost fell upon Adam, which beareth record of the Father and the Son, saying: I am the Only Begotten of the Father from the beginning."[51] Starting with Adam and through all generations of time, Christ's atonement would reconcile those who would repent, restoring them to the Father's presence.

Jehovah, who is Jesus Christ, revealed His gospel to the faithful in all ages by His own voice and the voice of angels. Enoch records, "He stood before my face, and he talked with me, even as a man talketh one with another, face to face."[52] He appeared to the

brother of Jared, to Moses, Isaiah, Nephi, and Amos, in each case teaching those mysteries of the meaning of existence that humanity has always yearned for, the very things we forgot by coming into mortality. For love, the Lord has wanted His children in all ages to understand and keep His commandments.

Thus, with the faithful in every dispensation Jehovah made powerful covenants, calling and ordaining them to His holy order, which is the priesthood. The priesthood gave them the authority to act in His name, to perform ordinances, to heal and bless and even "by faith, to break mountains, to divide the seas, to dry up waters, to turn them out of their course; to put at defiance the armies of nations, to divide the earth, to break every band, to stand in the presence of God."[53] So powerful was the faith of Enoch, in fact, that using this power, the Holy Priesthood after the Order of the Son of God, "he spake the word of the Lord, and the earth trembled, and the mountains fled, . . . and all nations feared greatly."[54]

Above: Straw brick remains at Tel Be'er Sheba. A well was dug in this area by Abraham. Water in the desert is a key to survival, with summer temperatures often soaring to 115 degrees Fahrenheit and above. A well becomes an extremely important focal point of a community. Wells of the desert are generally looked upon by Middle Eastern cultures as gifts from God and are to be shared freely with all in need.

Right: Looking north across the ruins of Tel Be'er Sheba to the Nahal Hevron (River Hebron), which flows only a short time during the year. From this area Abraham "rose up early in the morning, . . . and went unto the place which God had told him,"[55] to the land of Moriah, to sacrifice his son Isaac. It was on the morning of the third day when Abraham could see Moriah, a modern journey of about 50 rugged miles.

Living in the bleak desert of Haran, Abraham, repelled by his father's idol worship, sought the Lord in prayer. Jesus Christ appeared to him, saying, "My name is Jehovah, and I know the end from the beginning; therefore my hand shall be over thee." The Lord covenanted with Abraham that "as many as receive this Gospel shall be called after thy name, . . . and in thy seed after thee . . . shall all the families of the earth be blessed."[56]

With this promise, Abraham would become the father of the faithful, but how? At sixty-two, he still had no children as his wife, Sarah, was barren. Nearly forty years more they waited, yet Abraham "staggered not at the promise of God through unbelief; but was strong in faith, . . . being fully persuaded that, what he had promised, he was able also to perform."[57] At last the promised child, Isaac, was born, and one Jewish tradition says Sarah was so filled with joy that her skin became young again, the wrinkles falling away, and she counted her years with the age of her son.

After many years, the Lord asked the ultimate test, saying to Abraham, "Take now thy son, thine only son Isaac, whom thou lovest, and get thee into the land of Moriah; and offer him there for a burnt offering."[58] Moriah, a mountain whose sacred meaning would echo through time, would, according to tradition, one day be the site of the temple in Jerusalem. Abraham's feelings must have been anguished as he and Isaac made the three-day journey to Moriah. Not only was he asked to see his son suffer and die but also to replay a horrifying, repulsive moment from his past when he himself had been bound and placed on an altar to be sacrificed by a wicked priest. Now he was walking up a mountain to bind his own son on the altar. Apocryphal literature reports that Satan, disguised as a kindly old man, accompanied Abraham partway on the trail up Moriah, asking, "What kind of a God would ask this of you?"[59]

At the moment Abraham lifted the knife to thrust into his son and slay him, "the angel of the Lord called to him out of heaven, and said, . . . Lay not thine hand upon the lad, neither do thou any thing unto him: for now I know that thou fearest God, seeing thou hast not withheld thy son, thine only son from me."[60] But God the Father would not withhold His only Son from the world.

I stretch my hand over the sea, and it obeys my voice . . . I say to the mountains—Depart hence—and behold, they are taken away by a whirlwind, in an instant, suddenly."[61] This is Jehovah speaking, who in heaven and earth has all power, knowledge, and love. In His protective hands, "all things work together for good to them that love God."[62]

Jacob, renamed Israel, had twelve sons, the favorite called Joseph, who was hated by all of his brothers because of Jacob's preferential love for him and his spiritual gifts. When Joseph came to visit his brothers who were tending their flocks in Dothan, their envy had reached murderous proportions, and they took their seventeen-year-old brother and cast him into a pit. Not long after, a caravan bound for Egypt came by, and the brothers impulsively sold him to the group for twenty pieces of silver.

Yet it was not in Jehovah's plan for Joseph to be cast away and forgotten: "The Lord was with Joseph . . . and made all that he did to prosper in his hand." From prison, Joseph was called to interpret Pharaoh's troubling dream about seven fat-fleshed cows who were eaten by seven lean ones. With insight from the Spirit, Joseph said that Egypt would see seven years of plenty and then face a terrible famine for seven years. Advising that Egypt store wheat in the plentiful years for the lean ones, Joseph suggested that "Pharaoh look out a man discreet and wise, and set him over the land of Egypt." Pharaoh said to his servants as he looked upon Joseph, "Can we find such a one as this is, a man in whom the Spirit of God is?"[63] The prisoner of Egypt in a stroke was made second only to mighty Pharaoh.

The Lord had brought Joseph from a dry pit in Dothan to the throne of the greatest kingdom in the world so that he could become a divine instrument in saving the house of Israel. When the famine ravaged the earth and the people cried for bread, Israel and his house also sorely suffered. "I have heard that there is corn in Egypt,"[64] said Jacob to his sons. They went to Egypt and were saved, a type that would be reflected in the mortal life of Jesus Christ.

Pages 28–29: Valley of Dothan in the northern part of modern Samaria. In this place, Joseph's brothers conspired against him and threw him into a dry well. Note the perfect timing of the Lord: right after Joseph was thrown into the pit, the brothers sat down to eat bread, looked up, and noticed a caravan heading to Egypt.[65] Had Joseph been left to the elements and without water for long, he could have suffered greatly or even died of thirst.

Perhaps the glow of the burning bush by night brought the curious Moses to climb the holy mountain. Raised as royalty in Pharaoh's court, given education, wealth, and knowledge in the ways of the Egyptians, he had been outcast for his sympathy toward the Hebrew slaves. Israel, who had come to Egypt to be fed, had been turned to bondage by a new pharaoh who knew not Joseph. So Moses kept sheep in the land of Midian until the Lord called out to him from the burning bush, "Put off thy shoes from off thy feet, for the place whereon thou standest is holy ground. . . . I have surely seen the affliction of my people which are in Egypt, and have heard their cry."[66] Through Moses, the Lord Jehovah would deliver His people.

Yet Moses was concerned. Who should he say had sent him? "What is his name? . . . And God said unto Moses, I AM THAT I AM: . . . Thus shalt thou say unto the children of Israel, I AM hath sent me unto you."[67]

Moses learned more of the glory of this Jehovah when he was caught up into an exceedingly high mountain and "saw God face to face." As the presence of God withdrew from Moses, "he fell unto the earth," depleted of his natural strength. He said, "Now, for this cause I know that man is nothing, which thing I never had supposed."[68]

Who then parted the Red Sea that Israel could walk through on dry ground? Who fed them manna in the desert wilderness for forty years? Who gave them water springing from a rock? Who amid the thunders and smoke of Sinai gave the law? The Old Testament calls Him Jehovah. In mortality He looked like other men. It was Jesus Christ. Ironically, it was that very law that accusers would try to batter Him with in His lifetime. Some Pharisees would ask Him, "Why will ye not receive us with our baptism, seeing we keep the whole law?" But Jesus would say to them, "Ye keep not the law. If ye had kept the law, ye would have received me, for I am he who gave the law."[69]

Above: Glory of the morning sun flooding light into the bleakness of the Sinai Desert as seen from high atop Mt. Sinai. As one prophet exclaimed about the law: "My soul delighteth in proving unto my people the truth of the coming of Christ; for, for this end hath the law of Moses been given; and all things which have been given of God from the beginning of the world, unto man, are the typifying of him."[70]

View from a cleft in the rocks at the summit of Mt. Sinai. Surely the tables of stone upon which the law was carved were made of the red granite so abundant on the mountain. The first set of tables given by God contained a fullness of the gospel, but because of the people's wickedness these were broken by Moses, for the Lord said, "I will take away the priesthood out of their midst; therefore my holy order, and the ordinances thereof, shall not go before them. . . . But I will give unto them . . . the law of a carnal commandment."[71]

The children of Israel had been in Egypt for generations, but worse, Egypt had come to be in them. Though the distance from Egypt to Canaan, the promised land, is not far, they wandered in that wilderness forty years, that the searing heat, the struggle, the testing might strip every shred of the world from their souls. From the heights of Mt. Sinai, overlooking range upon range of twisted desert mountains, Moses had received the law. Unlike the law of Christ, which asked its followers to be anxiously engaged in a good cause of their own free will, the law of Moses was a preparatory gospel for those who neglect good works unless constrained by a law of performances. "The law was our schoolmaster to bring us unto Christ,"[72] noted Paul. Jacob added, "For this intent we keep the law of Moses, it pointing our souls to him."[73]

Thus, every morning and every evening a spotless lamb was sacrificed on the temple altar as a burnt offering. The priests were to keep the fire burning perpetually, its wafting smoke a continual reminder of the spotless sacrifice of the Savior. Year after year on the Day of Atonement, Israel was reminded that because of sin they had been cut off from the Lord's presence and therefore were subject to spiritual death. But God would accept a substitute—the death of an animal, perfect and blameless—instead of the offender.

As they trudged from one desert camp to another where crops would not grow, they gathered manna in the morning for food. It was a symbol of God's constant gifts to them, a sign of their daily need for Him. In one discouraging time when hunger and thirst had nearly overtaken them and the comforts of Egypt seemed more attractive than following an unseen God, they began to speak harshly against Moses, and fiery serpents came among them, biting with deadly fury. Finally, the people turned again to Moses, begging him to pray the scourge away. The Lord directed Moses to make a serpent of brass and fasten it to a pole, holding it up for all the people to look upon. "And the labor which they had to perform was to look; and because of the simpleness of the way, or the easiness of it, there were many who perished."[74] The serpent was a symbol of the Lord Jesus Christ held up on the cross, and the message was "Look to the Lord and live."

Survivors in the harsh, unrelenting desert of the Sinai must conserve and cling to every drop of moisture from the heavens. "Thou shalt remember all the way which the Lord thy God led thee . . . in the wilderness, . . . and suffered thee to hunger, and fed thee with manna, . . . that he might make thee know that man doth not live by bread only, but by every word that proceedeth out of the mouth of the Lord."[75]

33

The persistence of the acacia tree is impressive as it sends its tap root more than 300 feet into the earth to draw sustenance to its branches. The scriptures have been given to mankind to feed and nourish the soul and to bring us to Jesus Christ. Eusebius tells us that Moses renamed Oshea, the son of Nun, Joshua (or Jeshua, the Hebrew equivalent to Jesus) because Joshua bore such a resemblance to the Savior.[76]

Jacob, a prophet who lived about 550 B.C., wrote, "We knew of Christ, and we had a hope of his glory many hundred years before his coming; and not only we ourselves had a hope of his glory, but also all the holy prophets which were before us."[77] Though it is not always evident in Old Testament accounts, the underlying message of every prophet was the coming of Christ. The records contained a "fulness of the gospel of the Lord" when they were first given, but in the process of passing them down, some evil-designing people "have taken away from the gospel of the Lamb many parts which are plain and most precious; and also many covenants of the Lord."[78] In fact, the Bible refers to more than twenty sacred records that are not currently available in the holy canon.

Still, what remains tells us that Christ was joyously anticipated. Isaiah saw His birth: "Behold, a virgin shall conceive, and bear a son, and shall call his name Immanuel."[79] The prophets knew the plan of salvation and exulted, "O the wisdom of God, his mercy and grace! . . . O how great the holiness of our God."[80] Nearly 600 years before Christ's birth, Nephi described plainly a vision of His life of service and love: "I beheld the Lamb of God going forth among the children of men. And I beheld multitudes of people who were sick, and who were afflicted with all manner of diseases, and with devils and unclean spirits. . . . And they were healed by the power of the Lamb of God."[81] The Psalms passionately capture glimpses of His sacrifice: "My God, my God, why hast thou forsaken me? . . . All they that see me laugh me to scorn . . . saying, He trusted on the Lord that he would deliver him. . . . They pierced my hands and my feet. . . . They part my garments among them, and cast lots upon my vesture."[82]

In searching for a way to express His mission and atonement, the prophets called forth superlative names to describe Him. He would be Wonderful, Counsellor, The mighty God, The everlasting Father, The Prince of Peace,[83] a Star out of Jacob,[84] Messiah, Redeemer, "the Lord of hosts, . . . the Holy One of Israel."[85] The prophets said He would be born in Bethlehem, come out of Egypt, be called a Nazarene, have one to go before Him to prepare the way, and be betrayed for thirty pieces of silver.

Storm gathering over the Mediterranean Sea as seen from Mt. Carmel south of modern Haifa. Elijah came on this mountain against the 450 "prophets" of Baal and challenged them to prove their god. Their attempts failed, and Elijah prayed: "Hear me, O Lord, hear me, that this people may know that thou art the Lord God. . . . Then the fire of the Lord fell." Not only did the Lord show forth power here on Carmel, but this, according to Elijah's word, ended the three-and-a-half-year drought: "It came to pass in the mean while, that the heaven was black with clouds and wind, and there was a great rain."[86]

Now will I sing to my wellbeloved a song of my beloved touching his vineyard. My wellbeloved hath a vineyard in a very fruitful hill: and he fenced it, and gathered out the stones thereof, and planted it with the choicest vine, and built a tower in the midst of it, . . . and he looked that it should bring forth grapes, and it brought forth wild grapes."[87] This is the sad song of Israel, a vineyard, pruned and cared for, taught by prophets, and then bearing wild, bitter fruit. What a heavy disappointment to the Lord, who has so carefully nurtured the vineyard.

Yet the vineyard type is carried even further in the allegory of Zenos, where the story of a tame olive tree in a vineyard becomes an analogy for the entire history of Israel. The gray-green olive tree is a common sight in Israel, where it may live to be two thousand years old. With remarkable staying power, even when it appears to be all but dead, new branches will spring from living roots. So the story can be interpreted that the master of the vineyard (the Lord) nourished a tame olive tree (Israel) in his vineyard, but as it waxed old, it began to decay (apostasy). Loving this tree and wishing to do everything to save it, the master pruned it, digged about it, and nourished it, and though young and tender branches shot forth, the main top began to perish. "It grieveth me that I should lose this tree,"[88] said the master, and why not be stricken? The Lord had sent prophets, revelations, and signs, and still Israel strayed. Yet no effort was too great for the master to save his beloved vineyard. He grafted in new branches from a wild olive tree (the intermixing of Gentiles with Israel), hoping to give the tree new life. The master then took away the natural, young, and tender branches of the tame olive tree and planted them in the nethermost parts of the vineyard (the scattering of Israel), hoping that in other ground away from the decay they would yield good fruit. Thus, Israelites Lehi and his family were asked to leave Jerusalem just before the Babylonian destruction of 587 B.C. to resettle in the Americas. Though in this faraway corner of the vineyard, "they are not lost unto the Father, for he knoweth whither he hath taken them."[89]

Pages 36–37: Beautiful ancient olive vineyard near the fields where David used to keep the flocks of his father, Jesse, in the hills surrounding Bethlehem. An olive tree can appear to be dead and yet will still produce new life from the strength of the root at a later time. Trees thrive in the rocky hills without irrigation, able to endure long periods of drought. An olive tree can yield 25 gallons of oil each harvest.

Above: Early morning light bathes a hillside of numerous caves at Qumran, where records now referred to as the Dead Sea Scrolls have been found. Scrolls or fragments of scrolls have been discovered in the mountains pictured to the west. In ancient Jewish custom, one must never destroy a record or document in which the name of God is written. Parts of every book of the Old Testament have been discovered in or around Qumran.

The children of Israel lived in Canaan, the promised land, first under a series of judges and then under kings, most notably David and Solomon. These were the glory days for Israel, her greatest moments, with vast, secured boundaries. King David, who became a religious symbol of epic proportions, conquered Jerusalem and proclaimed it his capital. Solomon constructed the impressive temple with cedars from faraway Lebanon. He adorned it with gold and silver and installed the Ark of the Covenant in the Holy of Holies. After Solomon's reign, however, the kingdom was torn by internal strife and divided in two. Israel in the north, whose capital was Samaria, was the homeland of the ten tribes, and the remaining two tribes, Judah and Benjamin, formed the kingdom of Judah in the south.

Throughout this period, the Lord sent prophets as a sort of national conscience, calling the people to return to the Lord. Though sometimes their appeals were heard, this olive tree had decayed and to save His vineyard, the Lord would allow its destruction and scattering. Thus, in a three-year siege, Assyria conquered the northern kingdom in 722 B.C. Assyria's policy was to exile many of its conquered inhabitants to other parts of its vast empire. In this way the ten tribes became lost, many of them scattered throughout the earth's population. Next, looking for help from Egypt that never came, Judah fell to Babylon in 586 B.C. The temple was destroyed and the population exiled, but not before the family of Lehi was led away to begin a colony of Israelites in the Americas. Those dispersed Jews in Babylon lamented, yearning for their homeland: "By the rivers of Babylon, there we sat down [and] wept when we remembered Zion."[90]

The exile would end when Persia conquered Babylon and allowed the Jews to go home to rebuild Jerusalem and their temple. Yet it would continue to be an uneasy history. First the Greeks conquered them, defiling the temple by sacrificing a pig on the altar. Then in 63 B.C. the Jews fell an easy prey to the Romans. By the time of Christ's birth, they had known several conquerors; local leaders had been inept, greedy, and cruel. Despite their yearnings for a resurgence of a glorious nation, they had seen only turmoil, dispersion, and religious decay.

The Jews had become divided into various groups. The aristocratic Sadducees controlled the temple and the priesthood. The Pharisees interpreted the law for the masses, and its forms had become rigid and spiritless. The Zealots advocated armed struggle against the Romans, and the Essenes, whose Dead Sea Scrolls were found in this century, separated themselves into a remote desert location called Qumran on the north shore of the Dead Sea.

These groups were so far from the original spirit of the law that if someone were to come along and claim to be a new lawgiver, he would by their understanding be breaking the law. Instead, they looked for a great deliverer who would free them from the bondage of foreign rule and oppression. "Oh, when would he come? In the feverish excitement of expectancy, they were only too ready to listen to the voice of any pretender . . . Yet, He was at hand—even now coming: only quite other than the Messiah of their dreams."[91]

Looking east across ruins at Qumran where five different periods of settlement have been discovered dating from 150 B.C. to A.D. 68. A sect of the Jews— apparently the Essenes—lived here to separate themselves from the temptations and influences of Jerusalem and the world. The complete scroll of Isaiah that was discovered here is over a thousand years older than any other known copy of that sacred book. Reservoir areas for water were likely used for ritualistic washings, water storage, or perhaps even baptisms.

2

BEHOLD
THE LAMB
OF GOD

It was the time of morning sacrifice on that October day when Zacharias drew the lot for the hallowed service that a priest could perform only once in his life, the offering of incense in the temple. Bearing the golden censer, he stood alone in the Holy Place, and at the appointed signal he spread the incense on the red coals of the altar, letting its sweetness waft to heaven, a symbol of Israel's prayers and yearning for the Lord. No tradition is known of an ordinary priest receiving a vision in the offering of incense, but suddenly, on the right side of the altar appeared the angel Gabriel telling Zacharias his prayer had been heard and his wife, Elisabeth, would bear a son to be called John. He would come "in the spirit and power of Elias . . . to make ready a people prepared for the Lord." Zacharias wondered at the news; he and Elisabeth were old, and her barrenness had been the sorrow of their lives. But as a sign for him and all those who waited outside, he was struck deaf and dumb.[1] A new day had dawned in Israel.

Pages 40–41: Spring sun rises over the north shores of the Dead Sea in the Judean Wilderness. Near here John the Baptist was calling people to repentance and saying, "Prepare ye the way of the Lord, make his paths straight."[2]

Left: Original steps at the south end of the wall of Jerusalem which led to the temple at the time of Jesus. Zacharias and Elisabeth both were descendants of Aaron, and therefore any male offspring they had would hold rights to the priesthood. Thousands of people ascended these steps over time, including the Son of God.

Above: Detail of flowers coming forth from stone steps leading to the temple. For a woman to be barren in Israel was a curse above all others. As Rachel cried, "Give me children, or else I die."[3] Elisabeth had longed for a child, but hopes were dimmed by her age until that marvelous day when the promise was given by the angel Gabriel. John, by birth, would be a rightful heir to the throne of Israel.

How Israel needed the long-promised Messiah! Not only in the Roman oppression, but in the land itself, the absence of rain and dew, the disorder of society, the silence of prophecy, they needed their deliverer, but they had lost sight of who He would be. They looked for an earthly king who would come in sudden splendor and vanquish all their foes. What a surprise He would be to their dearest expectations. Nothing about the humble home in Galilee where Gabriel appeared was distinctive except the spirit of the young virgin Mary. And the angel said unto her, "Fear not, Mary: for thou hast found favour with God." She would bring forth a child, who would be the literal Son of God, and would call His name Jesus. "How shall this be, seeing I know not a man?" she asked, to which Gabriel answered, "The Holy Ghost shall come upon thee, and the power of the Highest shall overshadow thee." Mary's reply was one of trust and willingness: "Behold the handmaid of the Lord; be it unto me according to thy word."[4]

For comfort in her awkward circumstance, Mary traveled the hundred miles to the Judean home of her cousin Elisabeth, then six months pregnant with John. Who but one who had also known the miracles and mercy of the Lord could better understand her younger cousin's heart? At their first meeting, Elisabeth, filled with the Holy Ghost, needed not to be told of Mary's circumstance: "Whence is this to me, that the mother of my Lord should come to me?" And the babe who would ever be a witness of Christ leaped in her womb. A clue to Mary's nature is found in her response, a great psalm of praise to the Lord, whose echoes show she had a deep knowledge of the scriptures and the poetry of her people: "My soul doth magnify the Lord, and my spirit hath rejoiced in God my Saviour."[5]

Home after three months, Mary faced the wounded feelings of her betrothed Joseph. Betrothal was a contract in Israel as binding as marriage and he had determined "to put her away privily" until Gabriel came to him in a dream saying, "Fear not to take unto thee Mary thy wife."[6]

On a spring morning in Bethlehem, restless donkeys loudly bray, roosters crow, and the sound of tinkling bells play off the hills where sheep graze. Not in a frosty December but in a season of green, new life, Jesus Christ was born in an ancient, dusty village long prophesied as the place. *Bethlehem* in Hebrew means "house of bread," and He was the Bread of Life to a hungry world. Its pools of Solomon were a principle water source for Jerusalem, and He came to give living water. Lambs to be sacrificed in the temple roamed its countryside, and He was the sacrificial Lamb. It was the City of David, and He came, a Son of David, to be the King of kings.

So it was, with the spring flowers spread across the hills, that Joseph and Mary, both descendants of the royal line of David, came to their ancestral home to be registered for a tax ordered by their Roman overseers. It was a journey of eighty uncomfortable miles for Mary, now nearing delivery, and she and Joseph probably traveled with family to protect themselves against desert marauders. In Bethlehem, swollen with visitors, "there was no room for them in the inn,"[7] but another translation tells us more: "There was none to give room for them in the inns."[8] The innkeepers were distracted, self-serving; they had no eye for new stars or heavenly things. It was, as it always would be, a problem of heart. The very Creator of the earth could find no place here. Jesus later said, "The foxes have holes, and the birds of the air have nests; but the Son of man hath not where to lay his head."[9]

"And so it was, that, while they were there, the days were accomplished that she should be delivered."[10] Mary, that "precious and chosen vessel,"[11] "brought forth her firstborn son, and wrapped him in swaddling clothes, and laid him in a manger,"[12] in a stable for animals. Not for this birth would there be rich finery or skilled attendants, just a new star overhead for those who would look heavenward. Into the darkness, the Light of the World had come. He was, as Isaiah had prophesied, Emmanuel, God with us, come to bear our sorrows and infirmities, come to lift our souls.

Pages 44–45: Rocky slopes of the hill
country of Judea near where Mary came
to visit Elisabeth. One source says that
Mary's parents had longed for a child, for
her mother, Anna, had been barren.
Through angelic ministrations Joachim
and Anna were informed they would
bring forth a daughter who would be the
mother of the Messiah.[13]

Pages 46–47: View of Bethlehem from
shepherd's hill photographed on April 6 in
celebration of the true birth date of Jesus,
April 6, 1 B.C.[14] Spring is the most
beautiful time of year in Bethlehem. The
rains have come, and the hillsides are
covered with lush grasses and myriads of
flowers. Bethlehem in Arabic means
"house of flesh."

With sheep folded safely in caves scattered about the hills of Bethlehem, shepherds watched over them, alert for night dangers. Tonight there would be little sleep, for this was the season of special care when fragile, new lambs had to be protected. Then, out of the darkness, brighter than the stars, an angel of the Lord appeared to them, "and the glory of the Lord shone round about them: and they were sore afraid."[15] Calm came to their troubled hearts as the angel gave the holiest announcement that had ever come to the world. It was delivered not to the pompous or the powerful but to a group representing one of the lowliest occupations in class-conscious Israel: "Fear not: for behold, I bring you good tidings of great joy, which shall be to all people. For unto you is born this day in the city of David a Saviour, who is Christ the Lord. . . . And suddenly there was with the angel, a multitude of the heavenly host praising God, and saying, Glory to God in the highest, and on earth peace; goodwill to men."[16] With the shep-

herds would the hearts of people everywhere be turned to say, "Let us now go . . . and see this thing which is come to pass."[17]

The shepherds quietly spread the word about the child, while in the heavens a new star appeared. Wise men came from the east, following the star. Who were these men? Some have speculated they were Jews of the diaspora, living in Persia, who had pored over records enough to discern heavenly signs and their meaning. Innocently, they went first to the palace of Herod. They asked, "Where is he that is born King of the Jews? for we have seen his star in the east, and are come to worship him."[18] Troubled, Herod called the chief priests and scribes to ask where it was prophesied that the king should be born. They answered that it was Bethlehem, "for out of thee shall come the Messiah, who shall save my people Israel."[19] Then lying Herod told the men, "Go and search diligently for the young child; and when ye have found him, bring me word again, that I may come and worship him also."[20]

Page 48: Looking out from a cave in the hillside by Bethlehem at sunset on April 6. The young shepherd who would tend flocks in these hills a thousand years before Jesus was David, who, in his youth, was called by the Lord "a man after his own heart."[21] Perched on the highest hill just southeast of Bethlehem was Herod's magnificent palace and fortress, but the Son of Man would be born in a cave.

Above: Ancient manger at Megiddo in the Jezreel Valley. A manger was a feeding trough for animals and was made of stone—not of wood, as is so often imagined. Jesus, as a baby, was wrapped tightly in swaddling clothes and laid in a manger—and truly Jesus is the stone of Israel.[22]

The Nile River flows through Egypt, bringing the miracle of life to the surrounding desert region. Joseph and Mary and the baby Jesus fled Palestine by command of the angel and came to Egypt to live until the death of wicked Herod. All of the journeyings out of Egypt and the experiences in the wilderness of the house of Israel are types of the Savior's life and mission and of our lives as well.

To the glorious, golden temple Joseph and Mary came bearing Jesus forty-one days after His birth to present Him to the Father. The child Jesus, as the firstborn son of a Hebrew family, had to be redeemed, and Mary, having given birth, had to be purified. The wealthy bought lambs for the burnt offering of purification, but this family was poor and bought the offering of the poor—a turtledove or a young pigeon. Among the worshipers at the temple that morning was devout Simeon, brought there by the Spirit, for it had been revealed unto him "that he should not see death, before he had seen the Lord's Christ." Seeing the baby, he rejoiced and took Him into his arms, blessing God and saying, "Lord, now lettest thou thy servant depart in peace."[23] Then, looking at Mary, he prophesied, "A spear shall pierce through him to the wounding of thine own soul also."[24] Already, Golgotha cast a shadow in their lives.

Aged Anna, too, stepped forward to bear joyful witness that this child was the Lord, but in his palace not far away Herod was not so joyful. This promised King of the Jews was a threat to his power, and Herod's mad and frenzied history showed that he responded to threat with violence. "His whole career was red with the blood of murder. He had massacred priests and nobles; he had decimated the Sanhedrin; he had caused the High Priest, his brother-in-law . . . to be drowned in pretended sport before his eyes; he had ordered the strangulation of his favorite wife, . . . though she seems to have been the only [one] whom he passionately loved."[25] His three sons, the uncle and father of his wife, his mother-in-law, his friends, all fell victim to his suspicious and guilty terrors. Now he added to the pool of blood at his door by ordering the death of all the children from two years and under in Bethlehem and the nearby coasts, hoping thereby to massacre Jesus. Thus the revelation was fulfilled, "In Rama was there a voice heard, lamentation and weeping, and great mourning, Rachael weeping for [the loss of] her children, and would not be comforted because they were not."[26]

One apocryphal source gives insight into how John was spared: "Elizabeth also, hearing that her son John was about to be searched

for, took him and went up unto the mountains. . . . But Herod made search after John, and sent servants to Zacharias . . . at the altar, and said unto him: 'Where hast thou hid thy son?' And he answered and said to them 'I am a minister of God, and a servant at the altar; how should I know where my son is? . . . I am a martyr for God, and if he shed my blood, the Lord will receive my soul. Besides, know that ye shed innocent blood." Then they slew Zacharias "in the entrance of the temple and altar."[27]

Jesus was spared because an angel appeared to Joseph in vision, telling him to flee with Mary and the child to Egypt. The Lord had said of His people, "Israel is my son, even my firstborn,"[28] and because the Lord works in patterns, types, and shadows, the miracles, events, and deliverances of Israel's past were reenacted in the life of Christ. The prophets spoke of both Israel and Christ when they wrote, "Out of Egypt have I called my son."[29]

Ancient aqueduct that carried water some twelve miles from a source on Mt. Carmel here to Caesarea on the Mediterranean coast. Herod died a most terrible death, "swollen with disease and scorched by thirst, ulcerated externally and glowing inwardly with a 'soft slow fire,' surrounded by plotting sons and plundering slaves."[30] Knowing that no one would shed one tear of sorrow at his passing, he gathered all the principal families and the chiefs of the tribes in his kingdom to his Jericho palace and gave order that at the second of his passing, all of them were to be massacred.

Pages 52–53: Thirteenth-century arches on the temple mount in Jerusalem. The ancient temple was 162 feet high—a commanding structure on the 40-acre temple lot of Jesus' day. On feast and holy days, more than 100,000 people would gather about the temple.

When Herod was dead, an angel came to Joseph in a vision, saying to take Jesus and His mother home again. They settled in Nazareth, but every spring, joining with others in festive company and probably chanting psalms, Joseph and Mary went to Jerusalem for the Feast of Passover. At twelve, Jesus came along, entering the grand city Jerusalem, with its royal gardens and gleaming towers, its streets swollen with visitors, and the bleating of sacrificial lambs. Standing above the rest, in His mind, however, must have been the temple.

Wherever Romans, Persians, or Greeks went, they could take their gods with them, but for the Jews, there was only one temple in one place, Jerusalem, where the priesthood could offer acceptable sacrifices, where stood the golden altar and the candlestick shedding its perpetual light. Their history and their hearts were wound around the temple, and, in times of dispersion, the longing remained. In fact, "it was said that whoever had not seen the Temple of Herod had never seen a beautiful building."[31] Though it lacked the Ark of the Covenant and the Urim and Thummim, though the Shechinah, the Divine Presence, was absent, still Jesus acknowledged it as His Father's house and as His house.[32]

As Mary and Joseph left Jerusalem, they had traveled a day's journey before they discovered that Jesus was not in the company. After three days, "they found him in the temple, sitting in the midst of the doctors, and they were hearing him, and asking him questions."[33] The learned, whose lives had been spent searching the nuances and legal meanings of each phrase of scripture, marveled at the startling precocity of this boy, the depth of His scriptural understanding. How evident this understanding was during His later ministry as He taught others, saying, "Have ye not read . . . ?"[34] Somewhat reproachfully, Mary said, "Son, why hast thou thus dealt with us?" to which He answered, "Knew ye not that I must be about my Father's business?"[35] Perhaps already, as the boy Jesus watched the sacrifice of the paschal lambs, He knew of that Passover day to come when He, the Lamb, would be the sacrifice.

Above: Modern city of Nazareth in the Galilee looking to the northwest. Jesus grew up here and learned his father's trade of carpentry. Another translation suggests he was an "artificer" or "craftsman."[36] Surely He used this knowledge to later teach about a "wise man, which built his house upon a rock,"[37] and of another, who, "intending to build a tower, sitteth . . . down first, and counteth the cost, whether he have sufficient to finish it."[38]

Right: Light dances onto grass in a dry, stone wash just outside Nazareth. Surely the boy Jesus knew well all of the gullies, paths, and forests around Nazareth. Perhaps Messianic consciousness was touched as He looked from the hills of Nazareth to the Jezreel Valley, where the battle of Armageddon will yet be fought.

O f the upbringing of Jesus the record is significantly silent, yet it is certain that He was subject to His parents and was taught the ways of God. Likely at the doorway of their home was the mezuzah, a folded parchment upon which the name of the Most High was written, that reverence might be paid to it upon entering or leaving.[39] As a boy, He would have learned from the Psalms, "The Lord shall preserve thy going out and thy coming in."[40]

As a Jewish boy, His earliest lessons from the Torah would likely have been from the book of Leviticus, the particulars of the law of Moses. Here He would have studied about sacrifices, burnt offerings, the Day of Atonement. Could His own Messianic consciousness have been awakened as He repeated these ordinances? Was there a day, reading the scriptures, that He finally realized they were speaking of Him?

Luke said that Jesus "increased in wisdom and stature, and in favor with God and man . . . and the grace of God was upon him."[41] John saw that Jesus did not receive a fullness of all things at once "but received grace for grace . . . until he received a fulness."[42] In Nazareth, Jesus served under Joseph, "and he spake not as other men, neither could he be taught; for he needed not that any man should teach him."[43] Here He learned the trade of a carpenter. He must, too, have carefully observed the natural world, for His teaching would be laced with illustrations—the wheat and the tares, the lilies of the field, the habits of shepherds.

Being reared in Galilee was no compliment for a Rabbi or teacher of the law. A common saying of the day was, "If a person wishes to be rich, let him go north [to Galilee]; if he wants to be wise, let him come south [to Judea]."[44] Hence could a question of doubt arise, "Can there any good thing come out of Nazareth?"[45]

Imagine the tender feelings of Mary for her Son, for she knew who this child was. Still Mary "kept all these things, and pondered them in her heart."[46] "What marvelous and sacred secrets were treasured in that mother's heart. . . . He was hers, and yet in a very real sense not wholly hers."[47] "And after many years, the hour of his ministry drew nigh."[48]

There was commotion in the wilderness of Judea a full day's journey from Jerusalem. A man, not unlike Elijah the Tishbite of old, dressed in rough camel's hair clothing, was crying with a loud voice, "Repent ye: for the kingdom of heaven is at hand." The dusty descent of nearly 4,000 vertical feet from Jerusalem to the river Jordan was crowded with multitudes seeking this widow's son who was raised in the deserts on "locusts and wild honey."[49] John, who was filled with the Holy Ghost from his mother's womb, was ordained by an angel at eight days old "to overthrow the kingdom of the Jews, and to make straight the way of the Lord before the face of his people, to prepare them for the coming of the Lord."[50]

What a dark kingdom He had come to overthrow! In ancient times high priests had been appointed by God. Now Annas had been appointed high priest by the immoral Roman, Quirinius, and Caiaphas after him was appointed by Valerius Gratus. On the great altar in Herod's Temple, sacrifices were offered to the emperor and for the well-being of the empire. Absent from Judah was revelation, miracle, and prophecy. No wonder the people were stirred by the charismatic John preaching in the boiling desert! Some who taught them were self-appointed. John, as he acknowledged himself, was sent by the Lord. He preached with sweeping, renewing power to bear one anothers' burdens, help the poor, feed the hungry: "He that hath two coats, let him impart to him that hath none."[51]

To those like the Pharisees who rested their salvation upon their bloodline or their knowledge of the law and came only to see a spectacle, John said boldly, "O generation of vipers, who hath warned you to flee from the wrath to come? . . . Begin not to say within yourselves, We have Abraham to our father: for I say unto you, That God is able to make of these stones to raise up children unto Abraham." To those who had faith and brought forth the fruits of repentance by confessing their sins, John administered baptism by immersion in the water of Jordan and in Ænon, "because there was much water there."[52]

That day of days had arrived—a day when heaven and earth would meet. By eternal plan the Son of the Highest would now come to John to be baptized of him. John was the only legal administrator in the affairs of the kingdom then on the earth, holding the keys of the Aaronic Priesthood.[53] He was baptizing at Bethabara, "the house of the ford," the place where tradition says the children of Israel bearing the Ark of the Covenant crossed the river on dry ground to enter the promised land.[54]

The ordinance of baptism was common to the Jews. They saw it like this: as a newly baptized person "stepped out of these waters he was considered as 'born anew'—in the language of the Rabbis, as if he were 'a little child just born.' . . . The past, with all that belonged to it, was past, and he was a new man—the old, with its defilements, was buried in the waters of baptism."[55]

Still, baptism was more ancient even than Israel. It had been established at the beginning of time, for Adam "was caught away by the Spirit of the Lord, and was carried down into the water, and was laid under the water, and was brought forth out of the water. And thus he was baptized."[56]

Now, seventy-six generations from Adam, came the one who had instituted the ordinance. What a moment in all eternity to see, standing at the water's edge, this Elias and the sinless Messiah, who had no need of being cleansed. John, in reverential awe, said, "I have need to be baptized of thee, and why comest thou to me?" Then Jesus spoke: "Suffer me to be baptized of thee, for thus it becometh us to fulfill all righteousness."[57] The ancient prophet Nephi expounded on this moment: "If the Lamb of God, he being holy, should have need to be baptized by water, to fulfill all righteousness, O then, how much more need have we, being unholy, to be baptized, yea, even by water!"[58]

So John went with Jesus into the water and baptized Him by immersion. "And Jesus . . . went straightway out of the water; and John saw, and lo, the heavens were opened unto him, and he saw the Spirit of God descending like a dove and lighting upon Jesus. And lo, he heard a voice from heaven, saying, This is my beloved Son, in whom I am well pleased. Hear ye him."[59]

Pages 56–57: Flowers coming forth from the Judean desert in spring. John preached in these regions with multitudes coming great distances to hear and be baptized by him. The Lord's covenant with Abraham concerning circumcision at eight days old was tied to baptism: "that thou mayest know for ever that children are not accountable before me until they are eight years old."[60]

Left: The sacred waters of the Jordan River as beams of light stream from heaven. In a most literal sense Jesus descended below all things, for His baptism took place at the lowest area of the earth, 1,300 feet below sea level. The nature of the Godhead can clearly be seen on this sacred occasion, with three distinct Beings, God the Father, His Son Jesus Christ, and the Holy Ghost.

Above: Locust tree in the wilderness of Judea near Jericho. Seeds from the locust pod provide nourishment to poor people of the desert and were likely part of the diet of John the Baptist. These husks, too, were fed to swine and cattle as fodder.

Because the stern and impassioned John had caused such an uproar among the people, instigating a popular movement that cut to the heart of Jerusalem's puffed-up hypocrisy, some thought perhaps he was the chosen one, the great Messiah, who would redeem Israel. The Jews, therefore, sent priests and Levites from Jerusalem to ask John, "Who art thou? And he confessed, and denied not that he was Elias," but he also added, "I am not the Christ." Then some question arose as to which Elias he was, as their Jewish scriptures indicated clearly that one Elias was a voice crying in the wilderness to prepare the way of the Lord and another Elias was to restore all things. John clarified which Elias he was: "I am the voice of one crying in the wilderness, Make straight the way of the Lord."[61]

As the forerunner for the Messiah, John said plainly, "He shall come . . . to take away the sins of the world, . . . to gather together those who are lost, . . . and to be a light unto all who sit in darkness."[62] "I indeed baptize you with water unto repentance: but he that cometh . . . whose shoes I am not worthy to bear: he shall baptize you with the Holy Ghost and with fire."[63]

After Christ's baptism, John was bold, emphatic that Jesus was the Lamb of God. He had been told to recognize Him by a sign, and the sign had been given. "When he was baptized of me," said John, "I saw the Spirit descending from heaven like a dove, and it abode upon him. And I knew him; for he who sent me to baptize with water, the same said unto me; Upon whom thou shalt see the Spirit descending, and remaining on him, the same is he who baptizeth with the Holy Ghost. And I saw and bare record that this is the Son of God."[64]

John continued baptizing and preaching another year after Jesus' baptism, but now his entire effort would be to send his loyal followers to the Lord. "He must increase, but I must decrease,"[65] John told his disciples. Jesus would later say of John, "He was a burning and a shining light: and ye were willing for a season to rejoice in his light."[66]

Pages 60–61: Light shimmers across the waters of the Jordan River in early morning. John's call "was not a call to armed resistance, but to repentance. . . . The hope which he held out was not of earthly possessions, but of purity. . . . For himself he sought nothing; for them he had only one absorbing thought: The Kingdom was at hand, the King was coming—let them prepare!"[67]

Above: Time-honored site of the Mount of Temptation, where Satan tempted the Lord after His forty-day fast. If indeed this is the mountain where Christ was shown the kingdoms of the world, the lush oasis of Jericho would have been in plain view before him, with Herod's cities with a "grove of the best trees for magnitude" and graceful palms and fruits in rich abundance of every variety.[68]

Shortly after His baptism, "Jesus was led up of the Spirit, into the wilderness, to be with God."[69] He would be there forty days, fasting and praying, communing with His Father, seeking to understand the full import of His mission and of His Father's will. This was a tender relationship between the Father and Son. During His ministry, Jesus would seek His Father often, pulling Himself away from the pressing crowds, "continu[ing] all night in prayer."[70] One account says of such a prayer, "The eye hath never seen, neither hath the ear heard, before, so great and marvelous things as we saw and heard Jesus speak unto the Father."[71]

In this barren wilderness where the sounds of wild beasts filled the chilly nights and the temperatures could soar to 120 degrees during the day, Jesus fasted, not to afflict Himself but in a spirit of rejoicing,[72] sustained by an exaltation of spirit. Isaiah had written, "Is not this the fast that I have chosen? to loose the bands of wickedness, to undo the heavy burdens, and to let the oppressed go free, and that ye break every yoke?"[73] Still, at the end of forty days, He was hungry and physically weak when Satan chose this moment of apparent vulnerability to come to Him. What won't mortals do to appease the gnawing pangs of starvation? Esau sold his birthright; others have fought like animals. So Satan came to Him with taunting and enticing words: "If thou be the Son of God, command that these stones be made bread."[74] This was an assault on two levels—not only that He should use the powers natural to Him as the Son of God to appease His own appetite, but also that He should prove beyond any possibility of doubt that He was indeed the Son of God. At the waters of Jordan, God the Father had just called Jesus His beloved Son, but Satan was asking, "Are you really? Why not prove His love? Why not prove your worthiness?" "If thou be the Son of God . . . " Satan had introduced the doubt, using the same pattern he would use to discourage mortals through the generations of time, attacking their worthiness, their sense of mission, their sense of the Father's care.

Jesus was not deceived, answering, "It is written, Man shall not live by bread alone, but by every word that proceedeth out of the mouth of God." Next, the Spirit set Jesus on the pinnacle of the temple, and the devil came, saying, "If thou be the Son of God, cast thyself down: for it is written, He shall give his angels charge concerning thee: and in their hands they shall bear thee up, lest at any time thou dash thy foot against a stone." Again the implication of doubt, again from Christ the unflinching integrity: "Thou shalt not tempt the Lord thy God."[75] Then, from the top of a high mountain, Jesus looked over the kingdoms of the world with their wealth and splendor as Satan promised Him all these things if Christ would worship him. Jesus, as a mortal, may not have had memory of His preexistent state, when He had created all things, but could there have been a greater affront than to offer Him what was already His? Jesus later said, "Fear not, little children, for . . . I have overcome the world."[76] As one who had the attributes of both God and man, He endured and suffered the temptations common to mortality, and He triumphed, not only in these encounters with Satan but through a lifetime of temptation.

The southwest corner of the temple complex in Jerusalem. Although not traditionally thought of as the "pinnacle of the temple," if the Lord were brought to this corner and tempted by Satan to jump, the miraculous retrieval by angels would have been seen by thousands in the temple and in the crowded markets below, and surely the spectacle would have been taken as a messianic sign.[77]

Above: Flowers and grasses growing in the Galilee. Surely nature responded as the Creator walked among the flora and sat upon the rocks teaching the people. The Galilee was green and lush while Judea was more arid and brown. News of the Master spread with amazing swiftness to the regions round about Galilee, and throngs gathered to hear for themselves the Rabbi who "taught them as one having authority, and not as the scribes."[78]

Right: The path that the Lord would ask His disciples to follow would not be an easy one, yet Isaiah prophesied, "He will teach us of his ways, and we will walk in his paths."[79] Perhaps learning had overcome the Judeans, for their hearts were stony and hardened, while the hearts of the Galileans were generally more open and accepting of the Savior's teachings.

He has come." The word of Jesus spread quietly and powerfully, especially among the disciples of John. At first, it was a simple testimony of one person passed on to another. John stood with two of his disciples as Jesus walked by, and John said, "Behold the Lamb of God." Turning, they followed Jesus, wondering where He lived. "Come and see,"[80] He said. "Come and see": it was a refrain for all of Israel, for all humanity. We see Him with outstretched arms in invitation, "Come." Not come when you are worthy or come when you are perfect, not come when your life is cleared of distractions or pain, but come now, come as you are; arise, cast off your burdens, ye heavy laden, and come.

One of the two disciples, Andrew, profoundly stirred by seeing and hearing Jesus, went immediately to his own brother, Simon, and said with an excitement built of generations of yearning, "We have found the Messias." Come and see. The next day, the Lord Himself found Philip and offered the invitation to come: "Follow me." Philip shared the good news with Nathanael: "We have found him, of whom Moses in the law, and the prophets, did write, Jesus of Nazareth." "Come and see,"[81] said Philip. How much more readily the open-minded, robust Galileans would receive the invitation than the formalists of Jerusalem.

Nathanael came, and Jesus greeted him: "Behold an Israelite indeed, in whom is no guile!" "Whence knowest thou me?" the puzzled Nathanael asked. How could this Jesus know his heart, his thoughts? Jesus answered, "Before that Philip called thee, when thou wast under the fig tree, I saw thee."[82] This Jesus was also a seer, one for whom "secret things be made manifest, and hidden things shall come to light."[83] It was a witness for Nathanael as he confessed, "Rabbi, thou art the Son of God; thou art the King of Israel." Jesus replied, "Because I said . . . I saw thee under the fig tree, believest thou? thou shalt see greater things than these."[84] "I . . . know my sheep,"[85] Jesus would say, and indeed He did, whether under fig trees or in the fields. In the secret places of their hearts and souls, this Lord has personal, intimate knowledge of each soul. Even a sparrow "shall not fall on the ground without" the Father's knowing it. "But the very hairs of your head are all numbered."[86]

Bougainvillea growing in rich abundance in Jericho; it is used in traditional weddings for decorating and for adorning the hair of the bride. Tradition and scriptures emphasize the relationship of husband and bride with Jehovah and His people: "Thus the bridal pair on the marriage-day symbolized the union of God with Israel."[87]

At a Hebrew wedding, late in the evening, the bridegroom set forth from his house, attended by friends and singers, to get the bride and bring her home for a feast. The guests were given fitting robes, and the feast was filled with riddles and amusements. Jesus was in attendance at such a wedding in Cana when His mother, Mary, apparently having some responsibility for the festivities, came to Him because they had run out of wine. John the Baptist, fasting and garbed in camel hair, lived an ascetic life, apart from the world, but Jesus came among the people, associating with others in social friendship, a trait for which He would later be criticized. When Mary told Him of the wine shortage, the traditional text says that He answered, "Woman, what have I to do with thee? mine hour is not yet come."[88] That seems like a rebuke from this Son to His mother, inconsistent with His character. But another translation tells us better. He said, "Woman, what wilt thou have me to do for thee? that will I do; for mine hour is not yet come."[89]

In the home stood six stone waterpots used for the washing required by the intricate rules of the Mishnah. Jesus instructed the servants to fill them. Then He said, "Draw out now, and bear unto the governor of the feast."[90] Apparently without gesture or word, He had transformed the water brimming in these pots into an abundance of wine, at least 120 gallons. It was such a delicious wine that when the governor of the feast tasted it, he called the bridegroom in surprise. The best wine was traditionally served first, but "thou," said the governor "hast kept the good wine until now."[91] The Lord had provided generously as He said, "I am come that they might have life, and that they might have it more abundantly."[92] He is not a God of scarcity and austerity, making humanity scramble for their needs. He is the Lord of gracious giving and fruitfulness. This, the first recorded of the Lord's miracles, looks forward to the last when He will reign in a millennial time, a time of peace and plenty when even the fruit of the earth will yield "ten-thousandfold."[93]

Ancient stone waterpot in Cana of the period of Jesus' time. Such vessels held fifteen to twenty-five gallons. Mary's request of her Son showed her absolute trust in Him. Surely others, as they witnessed the miracle, began to build their faith and hope in the Messiah. The records do not indicate any "audible command or formula of invocation"[94] on Jesus' part; the servants simply filled the pots with water at his request and drew out the sweetest wine.

The first Passover after His forty-day fast, Jesus took a scourge of small cords and cleansed the temple, His Father's house. He healed, blessed, and taught, and He openly confronted the formal religious powers of Jerusalem. Gone were the days of obscurity in Galilee. Few could ignore the fact that this unknown prophet worked such miracles as had never before been seen in Israel.

These miracles attracted Nicodemus, one of the seventy-one members of the powerful Jewish Sanhedrin. "As a judicial body the Sanhedrin constituted a supreme court, to which belonged in the first instance the trial of false prophets."[95] This assemblage of priests and Pharisees traced its origin in the Mishna to the seventy elders whom Moses had called to help govern the Israelites.[96]

Nicodemus came to see Jesus at night, likely so the visit would not be known by his colleagues of the corrupted Sanhedrin. This government master addressed the Man of Galilee as "Rabbi," a highly respected title. "We know that thou art a teacher come from God," he said, "for no man can do these miracles that thou doest except God be with him."[97] Perhaps Nicodemus' phrase "we know" indicates there were other would-be disciples among the leaders of the Jews with less brave hearts who sent him as their inquirer. "It must have been a mighty power of conviction, to break down prejudice so far as to lead this old Sanhedrist to acknowledge a Galilean, untrained in the Schools, as a Teacher come from God."[98]

Jesus told Nicodemus outright, "Verily, verily, I say unto thee, except a man be born again, he cannot see the kingdom of God."[99] This meant repentance, baptism, and more. Born again meant having a heart that was changed through the Spirit so that one had "no more disposition to do evil, but to do good continually." Someone born of the Spirit would have a heart "changed through faith on his name,"[100] knowing "love, joy, peace, longsuffering, gentleness, goodness, faith."[101] Though Nicodemus was a supposed master in Israel, he could not at first comprehend the idea. Still, he became a secret believer who would later stand up for the Lord before accusers in the Sanhedrin.

Left: The glow of small lights illuminates a scene in streets of old Jerusalem at night. All the references to Nicodemus in the gospels remind the reader of his coming to the Master by night, likely because his discipleship had to be kept secret since he was a Pharisee and member of the Sanhedrin. Any Pharisee who believed in Jesus openly was excommunicated.

Above: Wind blowing through a field of wheat in the upper hills above the Sea of Galilee. Jesus told Nicodemus, "The wind bloweth where it listeth, and thou hearest the sound thereof, but canst not tell whence it cometh, and whither it goeth: so is every one that is born of the Spirit."[102] Jesus was trying to help this "master of Israel" come to understand the gentle but sure and powerful workings of the Spirit of the Lord in the conversion process.

Above: The village of Sychar at the base of Mt. Gerazim, a mountain holy to the Samaritans. It was some distance from here to the well of Jacob, perhaps two miles. According to tradition, Mt. Gerazim had miraculously been left uncovered by the waters of the flood and therefore, to the Samaritans, was the true place to worship, not the temple on Mt. Moriah in Jerusalem.

Right: Water container made in Hebron of the type and style in use during the first century A.D. A waterpot was a precious vessel to a family and provided for their daily needs of cooking, bathing, and drinking. The message of the Messiah to this meek woman was so moving that she left her waterpot and went to the village to tell all of her discovery: "Is not this the Christ?"[103]

The time was nearly noon when Jesus and His disciples arrived in a city of Samaria on their way to Galilee. The journey had been mountainous and long, and Jesus was wearied as He sat down at the very well dug by Jacob, the father of the tribes of Israel. Having sent His friends to the city to buy food, Jesus was alone when the Samaritan woman came to the well.

The Samaritans were hated by the Jews, considered "as a mongrel lot, unworthy of decent respect. When the Ten Tribes were led into captivity by the king of Assyria, foreigners were sent to populate Samaria. These intermarried with such Israelites as had escaped the captivity"[104] and began to change the religion of Israel to suit their purpose, saving some form of Jehovah worship but adopting rituals the Jews regarded as unorthodox. The Jews would take long detours around Samaria just to avoid contact with these people.

How surprising, then, that Jesus had chosen to come this way and that He would speak to a Samaritan, especially a woman. His smallest choices were always filled with meaning.

Water would usually have been drawn from the well in the early morning or evening, but this despised woman came at noon, probably to avoid the disdain of others. Jesus surprised the woman by speaking to her: "Give me to drink." When she wondered why He spoke to her, He answered, "If thou knewest the gift of God, and who it is that saith to thee, Give me to drink; thou wouldest have asked of him, and he would have given thee living water."[105] Could this man offer her something that would lighten her daily task of drawing water? He offered much more, a well of water springing up into everlasting life, "which gift is the greatest gift of all the gifts of God."[106] When He asked her to get her husband, she replied that she had none. Then He told her something that struck her to the heart. He knew that she had had five husbands and that the man she lived with now was not her husband. How could this lowliest of women be so well known to the Lord? "Sir, I perceive that thou art a prophet,"[107] she said. The Lord told her more in the first outright declaration of His identity: "I who speak unto thee am the Messias."[108] The woman ran with joy into the city, leaving her earthen waterpot and old life behind, and many believed her words.

The synagogues of Galilee had never heard a voice like that of Jesus Christ, and He came to Nazareth to teach the people. They all knew Him, for He had spent nearly three decades in this town, learning and growing, gathering with the others at the synagogue. "And, as his custom was, he went into the synagogue on the sabbath day."[109] Surely the rumors were already flying about some of the miracles He had performed, and His neighbors were curious to see Him again. The chief ruler of the synagogue invited Jesus to act as the Sheliach Tsibbur, the messenger or delegate of the congregation. Jesus would have conducted the devotions, starting with set prayers: "Blessed be Thou, O Lord, King of the world, Who formest the light and createst the darkness. . . . With great love hast Thou loved us. . . . Have mercy upon us, and teach us." Then the Jewish Shema or creed was recited by Jesus: "True it is that Thou art Jehovah, our God, and the God of our fathers, . . . our Saviour, . . . the Rock of our Salvation."[110] Here He was in their midst! What majesty! What power as He spoke these words about Himself! Then the minister delivered unto Jesus the scroll of Isaiah, for the custom was now to read passages from the Prophets, and Jesus began, "The Spirit of the Lord is upon me, because he hath anointed me to preach the gospel to the poor; he hath sent me to heal the brokenhearted, to preach deliverance to the captives, and recovering of sight to the blind, to set at liberty them that are bruised, to preach the acceptable year of the Lord."[111]

Then Jesus sat down, for now the custom allowed the delegate to make comments on the reading from the scriptures, "and the eyes of all them that were in the synagogue were fastened on him." He told them, "This day is this scripture fulfilled in your ears."[112] In their amazement some began to say, "Is not this the carpenter, the son of Mary?" "And they were offended at him."[113] Responding with great violence and wrath, they "rose up, and thrust him out of the city, and led him unto the brow of the hill . . . that they might cast him down headlong. But he passing through the midst of them went his way."[114] Jesus was not accepted in His own country.

As a Master in Israel, Jesus began gathering disciples—those who would learn His ways, do His will, and enter into complete fellowship with His work.[117] Jesus came walking by the shore of the Galilee and saw Andrew and Peter as they were casting their nets into the sea. He called out to them, "I am he of whom it is written by the prophets; follow me, and I will make you fishers of men."[118] In the Hebrew, this expression to bid another to follow was a permanent call.[119] "And they, believing on his words, left their net, and straightway followed him." The three of them went a little farther and found James and John mending their nets on their ship. These sons of Zebedee were partners with Andrew and Peter in the lucrative fishing trade on the Galilee. "And he called them. And they immediately left their father in the ship, and followed him."[120] Later, when the Lord asked them if they would ever leave Him they would answer, "To whom shall we go? thou hast the words of eternal life."[121]

Word of the teacher who proclaimed astonishing doctrine with great power spread like brushfire through the Galilee. He healed a nobleman's son and cast an unclean spirit out of a man in the synagogue where He taught, "and the fame of him went out into every place of the country round about."[122] People flocked to Him bearing their infirmities and sicknesses, their "diverse diseases and torments,"[123] and He had mercy on them. Wounded in the body or the heart, they came that He might give unto them "beauty for ashes, the oil of joy for mourning, the garment of praise for the spirit of heaviness."[124] At Peter's house in Capernaum, He healed Peter's mother-in-law sick with a fever, and at sunset "all the city was gathered together at the door."[125] "He laid his hands on every one of them, and healed them."[126] The next morning, seeking His Father, Jesus retreated into a solitary place to pray, but He was not to be alone long for Peter soon found Him, saying, "All men seek for thee"[127]—all needed healing for the bruises of mortality. "Sing, O heavens, and be joyful, O earth; and break forth into singing, O mountains: for the Lord hath comforted His people, and will have mercy on His afflicted."[128]

On another day while He preached at Capernaum, so many were gathered at the door of Peter's home where Jesus stayed that there was no room to receive them. To the crowd gathered at the door came a group bearing a man taken with palsy. Unable to make it through the press of people, but with a determined certainty that Christ could and would heal the man, they climbed up to the roof of the house, removed the tiles, and lowered the man on his bed to Jesus. Imagine the surprise of the crowd, the hands that would reach out to steady the bed, the upturned, hopeful face of the one who had been so long afflicted as his eyes caught the eyes of the Savior. "Son, be of good cheer," said the Christ. "Thy sins be forgiven thee."[129] But the Pharisees muttered among themselves, "Who is this which speaketh blasphemies? Who can forgive sins, but God alone?"[130] Perceiving their thoughts, Jesus asked, "Whether is easier, to say, Thy sins be forgiven thee; or to say, Arise and walk?"[131] The Son of God had come to heal both body and soul, and the people marveled as they saw the man leap from his bed: "We have seen strange things to day."[132]

Left: Uncompleted arch at Capernaum missing its keystone. Some Pharisees were so far from the spirit of the law that they could not accept or understand that Jesus could truly be the Messiah. "Indeed the whole spirit of their religion was summed up, not in confession of sin and in humility, but in a proud self-righteousness at variance with any true conception of man's relation to either God or his fellow creatures."[133]

Above: Six-pointed star found in the ruins at Capernaum, probably dating to the fourth century A.D. These two triangles, joined together, represent unity, lights and perfections. There is a Jewish oral tradition that says that the six-pointed star was engraved upon David's battle shield, and that the six outer triangles marked the six aspects of the Lord's spirit: "the spirit of wisdom and understanding, the spirit of counsel and might, the spirit of knowledge and of the fear of the Lord."[134]

The Lord had given Israel the Sabbath as a day of peace and spiritual renewal. Every seventh year the land was to rest to enhance its fertility, and after seven times seven the fiftieth year was a time of jubilee. But rabbis with furrowed brows multiplied the law, adding injunctions, restraints, and even the specter of capital punishment for trifling infractions. Thus some rabbis even held it as sin to walk on the grass on the Sabbath in case it be in seed, a form of threshing of the grain. Jesus the revolutionary did not come to be bound by hollow traditions or false formalisms, but to do "nothing . . . but what He seeth the Father do." At the synagogue was a man with a withered hand, and the Pharisees watched Jesus to see if He would heal the man on the Sabbath day. Knowing their thoughts, Jesus asked,"Is it lawful on the sabbath days to do good, or to do evil? to save life, or to destroy it?"[135] And He commanded the man to stretch forth his hand that it might be healed. "The Son of man is Lord even of the sabbath day."[136]

Left: Excavations at the site of the Pool of Bethesda in Jerusalem. Because Jerusalem has been destroyed at least twenty-five times, most of the original features of the city at the time of Christ are buried from twelve to twenty-eight feet below the present-day city. So thorough was the destruction of the "City of Gold" in A.D. 68 that the only thing it was left good for was plowing and planting.

Above: Flowers of Solomon's Crown are abundant in Israel and are a reminder of the splendor of the Lord's creations and of the nothingness of the kingdoms of men. A multitude "of impotent folk, of blind, halt, [and] withered"[137] would wait at the pool of Bethesda for a miraculous movement of the water that brought healing to them. On the Sabbath Jesus healed a man there who had been unable to walk for thirty-eight years.

The last light of evening touches a solitary spot on the top of Mt. Arbel high above the Sea of Galilee. Jesus could have come to this place as He sought for guidance, inspiration, and revelation from His Father concerning the calling of His special witnesses. The pattern beckons the faithful to find solitary places and to seek for blessings and direction from the heavens.

The time had now come for Jesus to organize His kingdom on the earth in the meridian of time, building "upon the foundation of the apostles and prophets, Jesus Christ himself being the chief corner stone."[138] He found solitude in a mountain apart where He could commune with His holy Father, for He would choose those who had been foreordained in the premortal existence to serve in this high and holy calling. He searched the hearts of those among His disciples to find twelve whose special mission would be to witness of Him to all the world. And Jesus "continued all night in prayer to God."[139] As the sun rose the next morning, He called His apostles unto Him. He ordained and set them apart by the laying on of hands. "Ye have not chosen me, but I have chosen you, and ordained you," He told them, "that ye should go and bring forth fruit."[140]

These were simple men, all Galileans save one; men who were not trained as rabbis or scribes but whose spirits could resonate with the words of life the Savior had to offer. Their names have come down to us as familiar friends: Simon Peter, James and John, Andrew, Philip, Bartholomew, Matthew, Thomas, Alpheus' son James, Judas (also known as Thaddeus), Simon Zelotes, and Judas Iscariot, the only Judean of the Twelve. "Ye see your calling, brethren, how that not many wise men after the flesh, not many mighty, not many noble are called: But God hath chosen the foolish things of the world to confound the wise."[141]

These Twelve, under the tutelage of the Master, would be transformed into powerful witnesses and would see visions, receive revelations, work wonders, and carry the burden of the kingdom of God on the earth. "Behold," the Savior would warn them, "I send you forth as sheep in the midst of wolves; be ye therefore wise servants, and as harmless as doves. . . . And ye shall be hated of all the world for my name's sake; but he that endureth to the end shall be saved."[142] All things would be asked of these special witnesses, even their very lives, for Peter and his brother Andrew would be crucified, James would be beheaded, and all would suffer a martyr's doom save the betrayer and John, for the Beloved desired to stay on the earth until the Lord came again.

With their holy calling, Jesus would give them the gifts He possessed and told them to "heal the sick, cleanse the lepers, raise the dead, cast out devils: freely ye have received, freely give." This would be the pattern for all the disciples of Christ. He taught them to rely on the Spirit, saying, "Take no thought how or what ye shall speak: for it shall be given you in that same hour what ye shall speak."[143]

"He that receiveth you receiveth me, and he that receiveth me receiveth him that sent me,"[144] "and he that receiveth my Father receiveth my Father's kingdom; therefore all that my Father hath shall be given unto him."[145] This was the promise of One whose promises are sure, whose word is truth and whose gifts are eternal. So these common men who started out as undisciplined, untutored children came "to the knowledge of the Son of God, . . . that we henceforth be no more children, tossed to and fro, and carried about with every wind of doctrine."[146]

Evening glow upon a lone tree growing out of rock on top of Mount Arbel, with the Sea of Galilee in the background. The cliffs fall over 1,000 feet from here to the lower hills by the sea. So honored and trusted were the apostles of the Lord that their very names will be inscribed upon the twelve foundations of the wall of the holy city—the New Jerusalem.[147]

3

THAT THEY MIGHT HAVE LIFE MORE ABUNDANTLY

From Mt. Sinai Jehovah had delivered the great law to Moses. Now, from another mountain, with the blue sea of the Galilee spread below, He gave the new law of the gospel. Where the law of Moses had focused on outward performances, actions visible to the world and easy to see, the new law focused on the state of the heart, the flow of the soul. "Blessed are they . . . " the Lord said again and again, not so much commanding His followers as describing the happy life, the way of true well-being. "Oh, the happiness of" those who are meek, merciful, and pure in heart. The "natural man" might believe he must compete for his share of things, oppress others, fight for dominion, protect his ego, prove his importance, and be ever wary lest another take advantage of him, but this was the way of misery. "I give unto you to be the salt of the earth," Christ told His followers. "I give unto you to be the light of the world."[1] He was teaching something far different from the world's frail lessons of success, of social survival of the fittest.

"Blessed are they that mourn,"[2] He said, or, in one translation of the Aramaic, healed "are those weak and overextended for their purpose; they shall feel their inner flow of strength return."[3] The Lord's love could be counted on without fail to heal the wounded and worn out. "Blessed are the meek,"[4] He said, or, from the Aramaic, "Blessed are the gentle . . . who have softened what is rigid within; they shall receive physical vigor and strength from the universe."[5] "Blessed are the pure in heart,"[6] blessed "are those whose lives radiate from a core of love; they shall see God everywhere."[7] "Blessed are the merciful: for they shall obtain mercy,"[8] "they shall find their own prayers answered."[9] The meek, merciful, and purehearted may seem to be the ones overlooked and trampled in a world where pride and ego rule, but evil is paid back in a heart filled with anxiety and fear, a running for but never finding satisfaction. On the other hand, the Lord offered the way to draw us out of ourselves, to focus His light within us, to give us peace.

Above: Traditional site on the north of the Sea of Galilee where Jesus taught the transcendent Sermon on the Mount. Jesus counseled His followers to lay up for themselves "treasures in heaven," not the things of this world "where moth and rust doth corrupt, and where thieves break through and steal."[10] He was teaching a condition of the heart, attained only by being rooted in Him.

Clover blooming in abundance at the site of the Mount of Beatitudes in the Galilee. Jesus taught in the most cosmopolitan region of the country, the main road of the ancient world. It was the meeting point between Damascus and the Egyptian frontier, between Antioch and Jerusalem, where the trade routes from Tyre and Sidon and the imperial highways all met together and branched out over the country.

Burnt offerings had marked the law of Moses, and now the new law required another sacrifice. "Ye shall offer for a sacrifice unto me a broken heart and a contrite spirit,"[11] Jesus would say. As an offering on the altar, true disciples must put their old selves, those complaining, protective, frightened selves that see the world through the blinders of their own will. The disciples must be transformed, born again, unafraid to render unto the Lord all that they have and are. They must not hold back even the slightest part of themselves, afraid of what the Lord will ask. As one disciple said, "I will give away all my sins to know thee,"[12] and indeed that is required. Just as new wine could not be put into old bottles, so a new society could not be built out of external performances.

Jesus asked that His disciples strip themselves of "jealousies and fears,"[13] that they strip themselves of pride. Two men, He said, went up into the temple to pray; the one a Pharisee, and the other a publican. The Pharisee stood and prayed thus: "God, I thank thee, that I am not as other men are, extortioners, unjust, adulterers, or even as this publican. I fast twice in the week, I give tithes of all that I possess. And the publican, standing afar off, would not lift up so much as his eyes unto heaven, but smote upon his breast, saying, God be merciful to me a sinner. I tell you, this man went down to his house justified rather than the other."[14] Jesus asked that His disciples sacrifice their self-righteousness, their need to create a worthy impression. They were not to do their alms before men, or to make a great show of their prayers: "Pray to thy Father which is in secret; and thy Father which seeth in secret shall reward thee openly.[15]

Where the law of Moses said one should not murder, now Christ said that His flock must sacrifice their anger, their contempt for their fellows, their enmity: "If thou bring thy gift to the altar, and there rememberest that thy brother hath ought against thee; leave there thy gift before the altar, and go thy way; first be reconciled to thy brother, and then come and offer thy gift." And not to your brother alone, but to your enemy as well: "Whosoever shall smite thee on thy right cheek, turn to him the other also." In fact, Christ asked the seemingly impossible, the complete sacrifice of will, of returning love for injury: "Love your enemies, bless them that curse you, do good to them that hate you, pray for them which despitefully use you, and persecute you."[16] His flock would sacrifice retaliation, vengeance, even taking offense as cankers in the soul they could not afford. Instead of focusing on the sins of others, they would look to shed their own weaknesses with His help.

"Be ye . . . perfect, even as your Father which is in heaven is perfect,"[17] Jesus said. In the Greek and Hebrew, *perfect* means "whole, healed, complete, the end product of a process." It was an invitation to joy, for only when we are whole can we be free. It does not mean that we always perform perfectly or competently, but that, repentant, we have no inclination to do evil, having been cleansed through Christ's atoning sacrifice. Christ's disciples must ultimately choose whether at the center of their souls is their own self-importance or the Lord, for "no man can serve two masters." We cannot seek both personal gain and the kingdom of God. Only when our eye is single to the glory of God will our "whole body . . . be full of light."[18]

A city that is set on a hill in modern times is the city of Nazareth in the Galilee. Though Jesus came to gather the lost sheep of Israel, He would not turn away any who displayed faith in His words. The Lord would give a charge to those He taught to be a light to the world and not to hide their testimonies under a basket.

"Consider the lilies of the field, how they grow," Jesus said to His disciples gathered on the hill. "They toil not, neither do they spin. And yet I say unto you, that even Solomon, in all his glory, was not arrayed like one of these. Therefore, if God so clothe the grass of the field, which today is, and to-morrow is cast into the oven, how much more will he not provide for you, if ye are not of little faith?"[19] Christ, the careful observer of an earth that had been created to bear record of Him, saw everywhere its lessons of our complete dependence on Him. He told His followers, "Take no thought for your life,"[20] a weak translation of the Greek, which means "to be very anxious about something."[21] They were not to be driven by fear, nervously trying to control all the elements of their lives. If, instead, they would make their focus the will of God, one day at a time, as surely as the flowers unfold, all things would work together for them: "Which of you by taking thought can add one cubit unto his stature?"[22] "Your Father knoweth what things ye have need of, before ye ask him."[23]

This, however, suggested, an abiding in the Lord, not an occasional visit to Him in times of crisis, with mumbled excuses about bothering Him. It is turning our lives completely to Him, because without Him, we can do nothing.[24] "Cry unto God for all thy support; yea, let all thy doings be unto the Lord, and whithersoever thou goest let it be in the Lord; yea let all thy thoughts be directed unto the Lord."[25] Hear this plea with a promise: "Ask, and it shall be given you; seek, and ye shall find; knock, and it shall be opened unto you."[26] Jesus spoke of a loving, intimate Father, ever concerned with His children: "What man among you, having a son, and he shall be standing out, and shall say, Father, open thy house that I may come in and sup with thee, will not say, Come in, my son; for mine is thine, and thine is mine? Or what man is there among you, who, if his son ask bread, will give him a stone? Or if he ask a fish, will he give him a serpent? If ye then, being evil, know how to give good gifts unto your children, how much more shall your Father who is in heaven give good things to them that ask him?"[27]

Wherever Jesus went, the blind saw and the lame walked, as the language of despair and utmost need always spoke to Him. He could read it in the face and the heart, and out of the infinite power of His love always came sympathetic response. If yesterday it was the healing of the centurion's servant, tomorrow it would be a new gladness, a fresh surprise, an unthought of possibility as He would say, "I have compassion on you." So on the road to Nain came a new gift, yet unseen in His ministry, this one to a widow weeping anguished tears for the loss of her only son.

Scholars have speculated that Jesus' own mother was a widow as no mention is made of Joseph after Jesus' twelfth year. Could Christ have also been thinking of His own mother and the loss to come of her Son, when He looked with such concern upon this twice-grieved woman of Nain? It was probably the evening, the time of funerals, when Jesus and His many followers coming from Capernaum met the grieving procession at the gate of the city of Nain. At Israelite funerals, mourning women would lament, musicians would play, and the widow would have probably directly preceded the dead, whose body would have been carried face up in an open wickerwood bier. The pageantry could have given scant comfort to this woman who had lost her only consolation.

Jesus saw her and, welling with compassion, said, "Weep not." Then He did what would have spelled defilement to a priest—He touched the dead body, but the touch of death could not render Him unclean. Jesus said, "Young man, I say unto thee, Arise. And he that was dead sat up, and began to speak." Here indeed was the Master of life, the one who could even awake the dead, and with love "He delivered [the boy] to his mother."[29]

Not much later, Jesus was dining at the home of Simon the Pharisee. Yet it is clear that the invitation had not come with any genuine warmth as Simon seems condescending toward his guest. Going against the customs of courtesy, he had not received Jesus with a kiss of welcome, provided water for washing the dust from His feet, nor supplied oil for anointing the hair of the head or beard. As they were lying around the table, their bodies resting on the couches, their feet turned away from the table, an unnamed woman, who was a sinner, slipped in the door. There was heavy

Light from the heavens filters through the clouds and touches the village of Nain. A multitude was following the Savior as they met the funeral procession coming out of the gate at Nain and heading eastward to the burying grounds. Jewish tradition called for all to yield to the bereaved out of piety and respect for the dead, but Jesus instead stopped the mourners and with love called the young son of the widow back to life.

prejudice against conversation with a woman of even lofty character, but to allow the attentions of a stained woman was unthinkable. Yet she must have heard the Savior promise rest to the heavy laden, inviting them to come unto Him, for she "stood at his feet behind him weeping, and began to wash his feet with tears, and did wipe them with the hairs of her head, and kissed his feet, and anointed them with the ointment." When Simon saw this, he said in himself that this Jesus must be no prophet or He would have known "what manner of woman this is that toucheth him." Jesus said, "Simon, thou gavest me no water. . . . Thou gavest me no kiss. . . . My head with oil thou didst not anoint. . . . Wherefore I say unto thee, Her sins, which are many, are forgiven; for she loved much."[30] When the Pharisees tried to trap Jesus because He ate with publicans and sinners, He simply answered, "They that are whole have no need of the physician; but they that are sick. I came not to call the righteous, but sinners to repentance."[31]

Thorns and thistles growing along the edge of a wheat field in the Galilee, choking the wheat. The parables of the Lord had a great power to reveal or conceal their message depending on the heart of the listener. Some came to Jesus only to see the sensational, and to them the messages of truth were hidden.

One spring day Jesus was sitting by the seaside, and such a multitude gathered to hear Him, He asked that a ship be brought near so He could preach from the water. These were eager hearers, some listening to learn and believe, others listening to find accusation. So Jesus taught them in parables, perhaps the most common teaching method among the rabbis. But His parables, unlike those of the rabbis, were filled with eternal verities meant to bring the listeners to God: "Behold, a sower went forth to sow; and when he sowed, some seeds fell by the way side, and the fowls came and devoured them up: some fell upon stony places, where they had not much earth. . . . Some fell among thorns; and the thorns sprung up, and choked them: but other fell into good ground, and brought forth fruit, some an hundredfold, some sixtyfold, some thirtyfold. Who hath ears to hear, let him hear."[32]

The listeners understood one level of what He said, many of them being "sowers" of their small fields, but the Savior wanted them to ponder and understand the parables beyond the obvious. In those days, the sower could choose to cast the seed by hand or by the means of cattle. "In the latter case, a sack with holes was filled with corn and laid on the back of the animal," so that as it trudged about, "the seed was thickly scattered. Thus it might well be, that it would fall indiscriminately on beaten roadway, on stony places but thinly covered with soil, or where the thorns had not been cleared away, or as on good ground."[33]

"Why speakest thou unto them in parables?" the Twelve asked. "Because it is given unto you to know the mysteries of the kingdom of heaven, but to them it is not given." Then Jesus further explained: "When any one heareth the word of the kingdom, and understandeth it not, then cometh the wicked one, and catcheth away that which was sown in his heart. . . . But he that received the seed into stony places, the same is he that heareth the word, and . . . with joy receiveth it; yet hath he not root in himself, . . . for when tribulation or persecution ariseth, . . . by and by he is offended. . . . But he that received seed into the good ground is he that heareth the word, and understandeth it; . . . and bringeth forth"[34] a bounteous harvest.

Above: The soil does not have much depth in the stony places, and therefore the wheat dies. Parables were a common mode of teaching in Jesus' day, but the rabbinic parables would often lead a follower only to further study of the Torah, not to introspective searching. For those whose eyes were blind to the truth, the use of parables was an act of mercy on the part of the Lord. "For of him unto whom much is given much is required; and he who sins against the greater light shall receive the greater condemnation."[35]

Left: Storks are a common sight in Israel as here among the fields south of the Galilee. Israel is a major crossroads for bird migration, with thousands of pelicans, egrets, herons, gulls, and ducks familiar to people working the land. The word parable means "to throw or set alongside or near." Most of the Lord's parables are metaphorical stories. The scriptures document more than fifty different parables used by the Lord to teach His listeners.

93

The kingdom of heaven is likened unto a man which sowed good seed in his field," the Lord continued. "But while men slept, his enemy came and sowed tares among the wheat, and went his way." Then the servants of the householder, seeing all the tares among the blades of wheat, asked the householder why the field had tares. "An enemy hath done this,"[36] was the reply. The actual tares the Lord spoke of were abundant in Palestine, likely the darnel, a weed that looks so much like wheat that until the time of harvest they are difficult to distinguish from each other.[37] "The field was the world," the Lord later explained to His disciples, "and the apostles were the sowers of the seed; and after they have fallen asleep the great persecutor of the church, the apostate, the whore, . . . even Satan, . . . behold he soweth the tares; wherefore the tares choke the wheat and drive the church into the wilderness." The Lord often talked of the great apostasy that would come after His ascension into heaven, and now He gave the warning in parabolic form so the disciples would recognize it after He left them. "But behold, in the last days, even now while the Lord is beginning to bring forth the word, and the blade is springing up and is yet tender, . . . the Lord saith, . . . let the wheat and the tares grow together until the harvest is fully ripe."[38] Even the farmers of today would never try to weed their fields or separate the tares until the time of harvest. And separation was necessary, for the grains of the darnel, so similar in appearance to wheat, if eaten would produce convulsions or even death.[39] "Then ye shall first gather out the wheat from among the tares, and after the gathering of the wheat, behold and lo, the tares are bound in bundles, and the field remaineth to be burned."[40]

A field played prominently in another classic parable. Christ said, "The kingdom of heaven is like unto treasure hid in a field; the which when a man hath found . . . for joy thereof goeth and selleth all that he hath, and buyeth that field."[41] Notice that he gladly sold all that he possessed to obtain this eternal treasure. "No man can become a citizen of the kingdom by partial surrender of his earlier allegiances; he must renounce everything foreign to the kingdom or he can never be numbered therein."[42]

Early morning light glows in a field of wheat and tares growing together in the Galilee. The appearance of tares is so similar to wheat that one cannot accurately tell the difference until the time of harvest. But the day of separation will come. The tares will finally be gathered in bundles and burned.

Above: Early morning light bathes the hillside where the temple of Zeus stands in the city of Jerash in Jordan. One of the ten cities of the Decapolis, Jerash was second in size only to Damascus in Jesus' day. Established in 332 B.C. by Alexander the Great, the city thrived for more than six hundred years. The site wasn't excavated until the 1920s. Greek influence can be seen throughout.

Right: Called by some "the city of a thousand pillars," Jerash is one of the most complete excavated sites of a Greco-Roman city in the world. Jerash was located on one of the major trade routes of the ancient world—the King's Highway. Jesus must have been well known here, for people from Jerash were following Him in the Galilee. While traveling "through the midst of the coasts of Decapolis,"[43] Jesus Himself may have visited here.

Jesus went about all the cities and villages, teaching in their synagogues, and preaching the gospel of the kingdom."[44] Then as now, in every season, the gospel of Jesus Christ is marked by missionary work, giving the good news of peace in this world and eternal life in the world to come. "Success attends his labors; multitudes hang on his every word; there is more ministerial service to be performed than one man can do. He can preach in only one village at a time; there are others who need to be healed, others who cry out for the cleansing of their spirits and the healing of their bodies, others than those to whom he can minister personally."[45] Telling His apostles, "The harvest truly is plenteous, but the labourers are few,"[46] Christ sent them out to gather the believers, out to the Decapolis, east of the Galilee. Wherever they went, they were His servants and ambassadors. One day the gospel would be preached to all people, but for now their charge was to find the lost sheep of the house of Israel.

The Pharisees hoped to excite jealousy between Christ and the Baptist, urging John's disciples to ask him piercing questions like this one: "Rabbi, he that was with thee beyond Jordan, to whom thou barest witness, behold, the same baptizeth, and *all* men come to him."[47] But John was not to be taken by such a temptation. Yes, he had lived a life of strict self-denial; yes, his ministry had been short and of scanty fruit; and, yes, now he was decreasing as Christ increased. But all this was as it should be. John's nobility of spirit is nowhere more evident than as he watched his followers begin to turn to another, and he rejoiced.

Now his trials would deepen. Herod the Great's vicious son Herod Antipas ruled as tetrarch of Galilee. Threatened at John's charismatic hold on the people, Herod threw him into prison. He was also boiling at John's bold denunciation of his adulterous marriage with Herodias, his brother's wife. John languished several months in a terrible dungeon at the fortress, Machaerus, near the desolate, forsaken reaches of the Dead Sea, while Jesus continued His ministry. Some have conjectured that as John suffered there alone, he began to wonder, "Why does not the great Messiah deliver me? Is He truly the One who has been prophesied?" He did send two of his disciples to bear a message to Christ, asking, "Art thou he that should come, or do we look for another?" But this was not an expression of doubt from John, but a teaching moment for his disciples. He had heard the voice of the Father bearing testimony; he was not a "reed shaken with the wind."[48] Most tender is this piece of information given to us in one translation: far from forgetting the imprisoned John, Jesus "sent angels . . . [who] ministered unto him."[49]

Meanwhile, Herod was desperate. He knew that John was a just man and "heard him gladly," but at his birthday, Herodias' daughter Salome danced, and in front of the chief men of Galilee, Herod made a foolish promise: "Ask of me whatsoever thou wilt, and I will give it thee."[50] She asked for John's head on a platter, and Herod delivered it, though afterward he would have night tremors about it. In the future, he would have the wretched dishonor of having stood in judgment on both John and Jesus.

Left: Sunset glimmers from the waters of the Dead Sea 3,800 feet below the site of Machaerus, where, according to Josephus, John the Baptist was imprisoned and beheaded. Herod Antipas was in the beautiful palace below the impregnable fortress of Machaerus having a party when he made a whimsical promise that led to John's death. From this site one can view geographically the whole life of John.

Pages 100–101: Hillside near the area of Bethsaida by the Sea of Galilee, reminiscent of where the Savior performed the miracle of the loaves and fishes. Here Jesus "fanned the flames of Messianic expectancy into a raging fire—here at last was the Coming One who would feed them as Moses (so they supposed) had fed their fathers."[51] Counting the women and children, the multitude may have been between twenty and thirty thousand people.

As the apostles gathered themselves together again from their missionary labors, Jesus, perceiving their weariness, said, "Come ye yourselves apart into a desert place, and rest a while," for so many were coming to them that "they had no leisure so much as to eat." Boarding a ship, they retreated across the Galilee to a city on the eastern shore called Bethsaida, but word went ahead of them, and many people running on foot along the shore arrived before they did, clamoring to hear the Master. The Savior's unending giving allowed Him little time for rest. A multitude of 5,000 men as well as women and children gathered on the grassy fields of spring, looking like a colorful garden, some of them no doubt pilgrims on their way to the Passover in Jerusalem. Jesus looked upon the wandering multitude starving for the word and was moved with compassion, "for they were as sheep not having a shepherd."[52] Their fathers had been fed with manna by Jehovah in the wilderness, but now they were without provision, a scattered flock.

After Jesus had taught and healed them, the shadows of the afternoon began to deepen. The apostles came to Him, noting, "This is a desert place, and now the time is far passed." They thought He should send the people away to buy food. Christ answered, "Give ye them to eat." What could He mean? How could they possibly buy enough bread? These twelve who had been with Him and taught at His feet could still not understand Him. Andrew saw a lad nearby who had five barley loaves and two small fishes. "But what," he asked, "are they among so many?" A barley loaf was the fare of the poorest, but the Lord took the five loaves and the two fishes and "looked up to heaven, and blessed, and brake the loaves, and gave them to his disciples to set before them; and the two fishes divided he among them all. And they did all eat, and were filled," with plenty left over, plenty to fill twelve baskets, plenty for other sheep wherever they might be.[53] Who was this man who could produce abundance at His touch? An irresistible impulse seized the people to proclaim Him a prophet and to "take him by force, to make him a king."[54]

Above: Before morning sun has touched the waters of the Galilee, the fishermen return from their labors of the night. When the Roman tax collectors came to collect a tax from the Lord, He sent Peter, the fisherman, to the sea. "Cast an hook," Jesus instructed him, "and take up the fish that first cometh up; and when thou hast opened his mouth, thou shalt find a piece of money: that take, and give unto them for me and thee."[55] Surely the tax collectors followed Peter and witnessed the miracle.

Right: Looking west across the Sea of Galilee as afternoon weather changes. Clouds can gather and wind can whip through the Horns of Hittim, blowing up a mighty storm with short notice on the sea. The Galilean province (about 60 miles long and 30 miles wide) in Jesus' day could have had a population of between 2 and 3 million people in more than 200 towns.

With the intensity and longing of centuries of oppression, the multitude wanted a worldly king, and they wanted him now. So Jesus "straightway . . . constrained his disciples to get into a ship"[56] to go to the other side of the Galilee while He went up into a mountain apart to pray. Would it be a similar crowd who would at His hour of need before a Roman tribunal one day proclaim, "We have no king but Caesar"?[57] For now this King of kings was alone on the mountain, while His apostles tried to sail across the Galilee. On this sea, fierce and sudden windstorms can sweep out of the steep mountains, hurling the ships about. At the fourth watch of the evening, between three and six A.M., Christ looked out across the sea and saw His friends "toiling in rowing; for the wind was contrary unto them." They had rowed only about three or four miles and were in the middle of the lake when Christ came to them, walking on the sea. He would have silently helped them and passed by, "but when they saw him walking upon the sea, they supposed it had been a spirit, and cried out."[58]

These disciples had already seen Jesus' magnificent powers upon the sea. Once before, He had been on the ship with the apostles when a great storm had blown up and the waves beat upon the ship until it "filled with water" and they were "in jeopardy."[59] Through the storm, Christ had slept on a pillow in the back of the ship until His panicked disciples had cried, "Master, carest thou not that we perish?" "And he arose and rebuked the wind, and said unto the sea, Peace, be still. And the wind ceased, and there was a great calm." Then the disciples had said one to another, "What manner of man is this, that even the wind and the sea obey him?"[60] Still, now they were astonished as He walked upon the water until He said, "It is I; be not afraid."[61] Peter, loyal and impetuous, cried, "Lord, if it be thou, bid me come unto thee on the water." "Come," He said, and Peter walked until the boisterous wind frightened him and he began to sink, calling, "Lord, save me." "And immediately Jesus stretched forth his hand, and caught him."[62] So He catches us all when we have toiled against the wind and spent our energy and would drown. Then He comes quietly to us with words of love, saying, "It is I; be not afraid."[63]

The expectation had grown among the Jews that the true Messiah would come on Passover to once again give them manna from heaven. The miraculous feeding of the multitude the day before had seemed to be the fulfillment of that expectation, and now the people, willing to give up their Passover pilgrimage to Jerusalem, returned to see if this was truly the Messiah. "Ye seek me," the Lord told them, "not because ye desire to keep my sayings, . . . but because ye did eat of the loaves and were filled."[64] "Do not work for the food that perishes, but for the food that endures for eternal life,"[65] "which the Son of Man hath power to give unto you."[66]

"This is the work of God," Jesus said, "that ye believe on him whom he hath sent." The people still wanted more: "Our fathers did eat manna in the desert. . . . What sign shewest thou then, that we may see, and believe thee?"[67] Jesus said, "It was not Moses who gave you the bread from heaven, but it is my Father who gives you the true bread from heaven."[68] Then the people said, "Lord, evermore give us this bread." "And Jesus said unto them, I am the bread of life; he that cometh to me shall never hunger; and he that believeth on me shall never thirst."[69]

Through the course of the past two days, the Lord had been trying to draw the people to Him by the symbols of the familiar exodus pattern of ancient Israel. Moses was at the mountain of God; Jesus had been at the mountain. Israel was led by God to the Red Sea; the multitude followed Jesus across the Sea of Galilee. Manna was called the bread from heaven; bread was given miraculously to the multitude. Israel had twelve tribes; twelve baskets were taken up of the abundance. Israel crossed the sea by night; the disciples toiled and crossed the sea by night. The Lord saved Israel that day at the Red Sea; Jesus came to the ship and saved them. All these things were a pattern to focus their minds on Him, Jesus Christ. But as His followers realized He would give them no more free bread, being blinded by their hunger for earthly food, "many of his disciples went back, and walked no more with him."[70]

W oe unto you, scribes and Pharisees, hypocrites!"[71] Repeatedly Jesus leveled a warning voice to this elect group of Jews. He had come to call humanity to God through humility and the cleansing of the inner vessel. The whole system of Pharisaic piety was in outward performances, often seeking to attract the attention and admiration of men: "Woe unto you, Pharisees! for ye love the uppermost seats in the synagogues and greetings in the markets."[72] Indeed, the desire for distinction among them during Christ's time was nearly insatiable. Ascending the ladder of ambition were the various levels of the scribes, rab, rabbi, rabban, rabboni, titles spoken with awe and a reverential kiss from young scholars who one day wanted to be like them. They believed that an oral law had been given to Moses on Mount Sinai to complete and explain the written law. This oral law had been handed down and preserved by the Pharisees, and they alone could interpret and expand its meaning. This exclusivity allowed them to adapt the law to new situations without admitting that anything had been changed. With the pretense of maintaining the law intact, they multiplied minutia and distinctions until the life of the Israelite was burdened on every side. In time, this oral law came to be regarded much more highly than the written law, and the Pharisee with his special knowledge was in a position of power. Yet, ironically, with all this pretension to piety, the Pharisees not only missed the Lord when He came among them, but they were also mad with desire to destroy Him.

"Woe unto you, scribes and pharisees, hypocrites! for ye devour widows' houses, and for a pretense make a long prayer. . . . Ye are like unto whited sepulchres, which indeed appear beautiful outward, but are within full of dead men's bones and of all uncleanness."[73] Like vultures, the Pharisees followed Christ, trying to prey upon Him. They interrogated, "Why walk not thy disciples according to the tradition of the elders, but eat bread with unwashen hands?"[74] Hoping to prove Him a traitor, they challenged, "Is it lawful to give tribute to Caesar, or not?"[75] To all of this Christ always had an answer. Though they claimed to work for the Lord, one day He would say to them, "Ye never knew me."[76]

Pages 104–5: Vast wheat field in the Galilee, where grain is raised in abundance. In the Middle East, bread truly is the staple of life and is often the only thing eaten for a meal among the poor. The common daily bread is patted thin and round, perhaps two feet in diameter, and placed in an earthen oven for only a few moments. The word for bread in Arabic is the same as the word for flesh.

Left: Archway on one of the streets of the old city of Jerusalem. The scribes of Jesus' day wrote out the law, and they also classified and arranged its precepts, counting with scrupulous minuteness every clause and letter it contained.

Above: Now-rare cedar of Lebanon cultured in a preserve in the western part of Israel near the coast of the Mediterranean. These trees grow straight and tall and were used by Solomon in building the temple. Because of their majestic look, they are sometimes used in the scriptures to personify pride. The tree can live to be more than 2,000 years old.

As Jesus sailed into Capernaum after visiting the Gadarenes, the people "were all waiting for him" and "gladly received him,"[77] but two in the throng had urgent needs. Jairus, the ruler of the synagogue, was probably a respected friend of Jesus, for in this very synagogue Christ had often preached, something that could not have happened without the local ruler's consent. Now this friend fell at the Savior's feet, pleading with the urgency of one seeing his child fade from life, "My little daughter lieth at the point of death: I pray thee, come and lay thy hands on her, that she may be healed; and she shall live."[78]

Jesus went with Jairus, pressed by the crowd on every side. Then "a woman having an issue of blood twelve years . . . came behind him, and touched the border of his garment." No physician had been able to heal her. But now, with a touch, "immediately her issue of blood stanched."[79] Jesus, knowing "that virtue had gone out of him,"[80] turned about and said, "Who touched me?" Peter noted, "Master, the multitude throng thee and press thee, and sayest thou, Who touched me?" But Christ could feel a single touch in a crowd as He could perceive the private ache of a heart. So the woman, ashamed of her malady, crept forth from hiding, "trembling, and falling down before him." "Daughter," He said, "be of good comfort, thy faith hath made thee whole."[81]

While Jesus spoke, some came from Jairus' house with tragic news: "Thy daughter is dead."[82] Christ, hearing it, looked upon Jairus' face wrenched with grief and said, "Fear not: believe only, and she shall be made whole."[83] Miracles are the fruit of faith, and Jairus had to hold fast to faith as they came to his house where already was the tumult of grieving—flute-players and "them that wept and wailed greatly." Jesus told the mourners, "Why make ye this ado, and weep? the damsel is not dead, but sleepeth,"and they "laughed him to scorn." Then, entering with the parents into the room where the twelve-year-old lay, Jesus took the child's hand and said tenderly in Aramaic, "Talitha cumi,"[84] meaning "Little maid, arise." And straightway, to the joy of all, she arose and walked.

flowing robes never runs anywhere.' To do so is humiliating."[97] yet as this son is still a long way off, the father, filled with love, ran to meet him and "fell on his neck, and kissed him." He gave him the best robe, put a ring on his hand, and killed the fatted calf for a feast so that all would be merry. When the elder son saw the festivities, he stubbornly refused to come into the house and complained. He had ploddingly, loyally worked for his father for years and had never been given a fatted calf. The father replied, "Son, thou art ever with me, and all that I have is thine. It was meet that we should make merry, and be glad: for this thy brother was dead, and is alive again; and was lost, and is found."[98]

The father, here, of course, represents God, and the parable demonstrates His amazing love and forgiveness. The typical scene would have been for a humiliated son to return amid taunts and jeers of the community. Yet the father protected him and turned mocking to rejoicing.

Built under Suleiman the Magnificent, these walls of Jerusalem date only to A.D. 1542. Jesus told of a king who forgave his servant a debt of 10,000 talents. Then, however, this same servant would not forgive the small debt of a hundred pence. When Jesus taught this parable of the two debtors, He tried to show the disparity between the debt He paid and the debts owed to us by our fellowmen. The ten thousand talents owed by the one debtor would be equivalent to over $4 billion in gold, while the other man owed one day's wages.[99]

Above: Living things springing forth from the desert of Perea in Jordan. What the Lord asked of His disciples was so unlike what the world seems to suggest one will need for success. The Lord gathered rough, burly fishermen around him and told them to be like little children. He taught His followers to love their enemies in an occupied nation with real enemies seen and dealt with every day. His teachings were bold and heart-changing.

Right: Late afternoon light touches the side of steep ridges that lead down into Wadi Qilt just outside of Jerusalem. The Wadi is normally dry, but in rare years a substantial river flows from here to Jericho for a few weeks. The gospel of Jesus Christ is like water in the desert, giving the powers of life to that which was seemingly dead.

Who is the greatest in the kingdom of heaven?"[100] "Which of them should be accounted the greatest?"[101] These were questions that would be raised more than once among the disciples of Jesus, a question based on a most worldly impulse—who is number one? "Pride gets no pleasure out of having something, only out of having more of it than the next man. . . . It is the comparison that makes you proud: the pleasure of being above the rest."[102] Pride was not to be the principle upon which the kingdom of heaven was founded. "Who is the greatest in the kingdom of heaven?" Jesus had an answer for His disciples, who were still maturing in understanding. He "called a little child unto him, and set him in the midst of them. "Whosoever shall humble himself as this little child," He said, "the same is greatest in the kingdom of heaven."[103] Each was to become "as a child, submissive, meek, humble, patient, full of love, willing to submit to all things which the Lord seeth fit to inflict upon him, even as a child doth submit to his father."[104]

If they were to hear the glorious words "Come, ye blessed of my Father, inherit the kingdom prepared for you from the foundation of the world," they must seek not to be the chief but rather the servant of all. Jesus said: "For I was an hungred, and ye gave me meat: I was thirsty, and ye gave me drink: I was a stranger, and ye took me in: naked, and ye clothed me: I was sick, and ye visited me: I was in prison, and ye came unto me. Then shall the righteous answer him, saying, Lord, when saw we thee an hungred, and fed thee? or thirsty, and gave thee drink? When saw we thee a stranger, and took thee in? or naked, and clothed thee? Or when saw we thee sick, or in prison, and came unto thee? And the King shall answer and say unto them, Verily I say unto you, Inasmuch as ye have done it unto one of the least of these my brethren, ye have done it unto me."[105]

Rather than seeking to raise himself above his brother, a true disciple would "esteem his brother as himself, and practice virtue and holiness before me. . . . For what man among you having twelve sons" would say unto one: "Be thou clothed in robes and sit thou here; and to the other: Be thou clothed in rags and sit thou there? . . . I say unto you, be one; and if ye are not one ye are not mine."[106]

The year from the Passover after the feeding of the 5,000 to the Passover when Christ was killed marked a period of decline of popular opinion toward Him. Before, some scribes and Pharisees with their devious questions had despised Him, but many of the multitude had loved Him, basking with gladness in His teachings and miracles. However, after the bread of life sermon and His refusal to step forth as earthly king, His popularity began to wane. He spoke what seemed to be hard things to a people so long oppressed: become as a child, love your enemies, seek a peace that is not of this world.

When Jesus took His apostles on a missionary journey inland to Caesarea Phillipi, He was an outcast from Galilee. Many had been told that He had performed His miracles through the power of the devil. Amid such widespread defection, He felt to bear testimony.

At Caesarea Phillipi, He asked, "Whom do men say that I the Son of man am?"[107] The answer was embedded in the question. He was the Son of the Man of Holiness, who is God, the Eternal Father. Jesus Christ is His firstborn.

The disciples passed on what they had heard. Some people, like fearful, superstitious Herod Antipas, thought Jesus was John the Baptist risen from the dead. Some thought He was that Elias, so prominent in Jewish scripture, who would restore all things. Others believed Him to be one of the old prophets come again. Then Christ asked his intimate friends, "But whom say ye that I am?" Peter affirmed without hesitation, "Thou art the Christ, the Son of the living God." Jesus responded, "Blessed art thou, . . . for flesh and blood hath not revealed it unto thee, but my Father which is in heaven."[108]

Peter had been given revelation, an undying knowledge that Jesus was the Christ. Upon such revelation, this steady, unmoving rock of testimony of His divinity, would the Lord build His church, "and the gates of hell shall not prevail against it."[109] Peter was then promised that he would be given the keys of the kingdom, the priesthood power and authority to act in the name of the Lord.

Evening was upon them as Jesus took His chief apostles, Peter, James, and John, "into an high mountain apart."[110] As He climbed these slopes, what solemn thoughts may have filled His heart, for He had come to commune with His Father, and perhaps to receive the sweet ministrations of heaven to prepare and fortify Him for His coming atonement and death. The apostles, too, would need this hour of vision and comfort to prepare their hearts to stand unshaken before the shameful insults and awful humiliation in the days to come.

After they arrived at their solitary place, the exhausted apostles slept while Jesus prayed and received the comfort and reassurance He needed from His Father. Even in Gethsemane itself He would need angelic assistance to face the terrors and anguish of the atonement until that time when He was left alone to triumph over sin. When the apostles awoke, they saw and heard unspeakable things, such as is rarely given to mortals. In their descriptions, they struggle for words. Christ was transfigured before them, "and his face did shine as the sun, and his raiment was white as the light."[111] His clothes were "white and glittering,"[112] "exceeding white as snow."[113]

Then, quickened by the Spirit, the apostles saw two beings who while on earth had been translated for the job they were about to perform. These were Moses and Elijah, who appeared in glory to speak of Christ's death and resurrection. Just days earlier, Jesus had explained to His disciples that He must "suffer many things, and be rejected of the elders and chief priests and scribes, and be slain and be raised the third day,"[114] to which Peter had adamantly protested, "Lord, this shall not be unto thee."[115] Now, with the added testimony of these heavenly ministrants, Peter was assured it must be so.

Christ had promised Peter the keys of the kingdom of heaven, saying, "Whatsoever thou shalt bind on earth shall be bound in heaven."[116] Moses and Elijah now conferred these priesthood keys upon the apostles. Yet this was not the end of the night's wonders, for a bright cloud overshadowed them, shielding the face and form of God the Father, who said, "This is my beloved Son, in whom I am well pleased; hear ye him."[117]

Pages 116–17: Massive rock cliffs at Caesarea Philippi with one of the main sources of water for Israel freely flowing from beneath it. The Lord significantly used a subtle word play on Peter's name here, for petros *means "small rock" and* petra *means "bedrock." Christ is the Stone of Israel, and Jesus, likely standing by this rock face, emphasized the powerful rock upon which the church would be established: the rock of revelation.*

Left: Morning sun bursts forth in splendor through clouds above Mt. Tabor in the Jezreel Valley, a possible site for the transfiguration of Jesus. Mt. Hermon, in the north, is another site thought to be the location of this grand event. One translation indicates that Elias (John the Baptist) was here at the event. The pattern of the transfiguration of the earth was shown to the apostles in this glorious vision, "of which account the fulness ye have not yet received."[118]

Sun touches the top of the Herodian wall at south end of the temple complex in Jerusalem. When Peter asked the Lord, "How oft shall my brother sin against me, and I forgive him?" the Lord answered with a resounding "Seventy times seven!"[119] Then in modern revelation He added, "I, the Lord, will forgive whom I will forgive, but of you it is required to forgive all men."[120]

It was an October morning in Jerusalem during the Feast of Tabernacles when Jesus sat in the temple teaching. The celebrating crowds had been divided the day before because of Him. Some had said, "This is the Prophet"; some, "This is the Christ," infuriating the chief priests. Yet even their own officers would not bring Him to them, saying, "Never man spake like this man."[121] Thus, during the night, the Jewish rulers wove a net to entangle Him.

As He taught, they brought to Him a woman who had been taken in the very act of adultery, probably caught in the immorality and abandonment of the feast. Imagine the terror-stricken woman, fresh from the agony of detection, dragged before the pitiless faces of the people and flung into the sacred grounds of the temple. Was she still scantily clothed, bruised from her rough handling? Was she set before the Lord or thrown there in contempt? Apparently her accusers were not interested in her. They had brought her to Jesus because they hated Him. Then they asked the question they hoped would ensnare Him: "Master, this woman was taken in adultery, in the very act. Now Moses in the law commanded us, that such should be stoned: but what sayest thou?"[122]

As the woman trembled before Him, they thought they had caught Him in a dilemma. Everyone knew that the law of Moses decreed death for adulterers, both men and women, and that the accuser should cast the first stone. If Jesus excused the woman, it would seem He was denying the law. If, however, He condemned her, where was the compassion and forgiveness that had marked His ministry? He ate with sinners; He had chosen a publican among His Twelve. How would He treat the adulteress?

In the face of their hypocrisy, Christ gave the perfect response—nothing. He just "stooped down, and with his finger wrote on the ground, as though he heard them not." Was this a reminder that He had first given them the law, written with His own finger on Moses' stone tablets? Or, very different, was it a reminder that what was written in dust could be swept away with the wind? As they continued to question Him, He stood and said, "He that is without sin among you, let him first cast a stone at her."[123] Was he

speaking not just of sin in general but more stingingly of this same sin? "Which among you is not an adulterer?"

The question seared their shame-ridden hearts, those who would stone a woman when they themselves were impure. "And they which heard it, being convicted by their own conscience, went out one by one, beginning at the eldest even unto the last: and Jesus was left alone, and the woman standing in the midst." When Jesus saw they were alone, He said, "Woman, where are those thine accusers? hath no man condemned thee?" She said, "No man, Lord." And Jesus said unto her, "Neither do I condemn thee: go, and sin no more."[124] The gratitude and release from bondage she felt at His words could only be expressed in her life: "The woman glorified God from that hour, and believed."[125] It is God's forgiving love that frees us from guilt and pain: "Behold, he who has repented of his sins, the same is forgiven, and I, the Lord remember them no more."[126]

Detail of giant blocks of stone weighing three to four tons each in the south wall of the temple complex dating to the time of Jesus. The woman left the scene and became numbered among the believers. "By this ye may know," the Lord emphasizes, "if a man repenteth of his sins—behold, he will confess them and forsake them."[127]

As the crowds on the temple mount continued to question Jesus about who He was, He said something that must have pierced them to the heart. Through their years of dispersion and subjugation, they had tenaciously held to their chosen status. They were the seed of Abraham, God's elect, a designation many wore with a strutting pride. Now Christ challenged that saying: "If ye were Abraham's children, ye would do the works of Abraham" but instead "ye seek to kill me, because my word hath no place in you." "Your father Abraham rejoiced to see my day: and he saw it, and was glad." Only those who accepted Him would be heir to God's blessings. He could not have spoken more plainly: "Verily, verily, I say unto you, Before Abraham was, I am."[128] Many listeners knew He referred to the Lord's naming Himself before Moses "I AM THAT I AM."[129] This Jesus was proclaiming Himself the great Jehovah who had given the law from Sinai. Infuriated at the supposed blasphemy, the people took up stones to cast them at Him, but His hour had not yet come.

Left: Light touches the terraced fields so typical of the Holy Land near Hebron. Generations of stone removal and careful husbandry have made these otherwise sterile areas quite fertile. The rains often come in torrents for a short time each year, so the leveling of the hills helps hold the precious moisture.

Above: Tomb of the Patriarchs at Hebron built by Herod the Great over the cave of Machpelah. Here Abraham and Sarah, Isaac and Rebekah, and Jacob and Leah were entombed. While thousands come to see where these were buried, modern revelation says that "they have entered into their exaltation, according to the promises, and sit upon thrones, and are not angels but are gods."[130]

123

Aman blind from birth was begging on the Sabbath, probably on the temple mount, when Jesus' disciples asked, "Master, who did sin, this man, or his parents, that he was born blind?" It was a typical question for those who had been reared to believe that disease was punishment for sin. A common Jewish view held that even the unrighteous thoughts of a mother might affect the state of her unborn child. Jesus' answer was thus surprising: "Neither hath this man sinned, nor his parents: but that the works of God should be made manifest in him."[131] Then the Savior anointed the man's eyes with clay and asked him to go wash in the nearby pool of Siloam, and the man obeyed and went away with his eyes opened.

His neighbors, probably accustomed to the familiar sight of the beggar, marveled that the blind now saw, and immediately they went to some Pharisees, who brought the man forward for an inquisition, hoping to find a charge against Christ. The testimony of the man was straightforward: "He put clay upon mine eyes, and I washed, and do see." The wonder of it could neither be denied nor explained, and in a turn the Pharisaic view was itself on trial. If this Jesus acted by the power of God, then the divinity of their own Sabbath rules, the power of their position itself, was in question. Unthinkable. Next they brought in his parents to verify that the man had indeed been born blind. This they could not deny, but they gave an evasive answer when asked how he had been cured. They knew "that if any man did confess that [Jesus] was Christ, he should be put out of the synagogue."[132]

Excommunication, depending on the degree, meant a sort of living death for the people. The excommunicant "would allow his beard and hair to grow wild and shaggy; he would not bathe, nor anoint himself. . . . As if he were a leper, people would keep at a distance of four cubits from him."[133] Even before this threat of the Sanhedrin, the healed man did not cower: "If this man were not of God, he could do nothing." So the Sanhedrin cast him out, but Jesus came to him, testifying that He was the Son of God, and the man answered, "Lord, I believe."[134] That day the blind truly saw, and the sighted Sanhedrin proved blind.

Burned black in the sun, roaming the rocky hills in every kind of weather, the Middle Eastern shepherd has a tender relationship with his flock. He knows each one; each has a name. If one is stuck in a rocky, mountain crag, he will leave the others to find it, carrying it back, cradled protectively against his body. At night, when creatures roam the desert, hungry for sheep who have no defense against predators, the shepherd protects them in a fold. A hireling might flee before a wolf, leaving the sheep defenseless, but not the good shepherd. He would even give his life for his sheep. In the morning, he comes to the door of the sheepfold and calls his own sheep by name. Even if it is a common fold where other flocks have been sheltered, his sheep hear his voice and follow him, for they know him. They do not respond to the voice of strangers.

In modern times a man traveling in a Middle-Eastern desert came upon a sheep that had been hit and injured by the king's car. An old shepherd, with a flock of fifteen or twenty, listened as the man explained to him that by law the shepherd must be compensated one hundred times the value of the sheep. However, under the same law, the injured sheep must be slain and the meat divided among the people. The traveler was told, "The old shepherd will not accept the money. They never do." When he asked why, it was explained, "Because of the love he has for each of his sheep." At that, the old shepherd reached down, lifted the injured lamb, and placed it in a pouch on the front of his robe. He stroked the sheep's head again and again, repeating his name as he walked off into the desert.[138]

"I am the good shepherd," said the Lord, "and know my sheep. . . . My sheep hear my voice, . . . and they follow me."[139] To His listeners who lived in a land of shepherds, it was a compelling image: "The Lord is my shepherd; I shall not want." As a lamb, He leads me to green pastures and still waters, to all that is nourishing and protecting. When I am broken, "He restoreth my soul." Though I walk through the deepest darkness, "I will fear no evil: for thou art with me." Only because of the good shepherd "goodness and mercy shall follow me all the days of my life."[140]

Pages 124–25: Western wall of the temple complex of Jerusalem, the holiest spot in the world to the Jews. A common solicitation for alms in the days of Jesus was, "O tenderhearted, by me gain merit, to thine own benefit."[135] And Jesus did not turn the blind away. The Pharisees exclaimed, "Since the world began was it not heard that any man opened the eyes of one that was born blind, except he be of God."[136]

Above: Last light of afternoon gently warms the backs of sheep in the hills around Bethlehem in Judea. The prophet Benjamin taught: "Whosoever should believe that Christ should come, the same might receive remission of their sins, and rejoice with exceedingly great joy, even as though he had already come among them."[137]

Right: Sheep grazing in the hills around Bethlehem just before the shepherd calls them into the fold. Sheep are defenseless against the wolves and lions of the desert and must have constant care. The sheep know the shepherd and are truly known of him, each one individually.

A deep doctrinal discussion was in progress, and the disciples thought Jesus was too busy when the little children were brought to Him. He was not to be disturbed, they said, responding out of the Jewish practice and tradition that kept women and children in the background. But the Savior was much displeased at this and said, "Suffer the little children to come unto me, and forbid them not: for of such is the kingdom of God."[141] What a moment of surpassing sweetness this was as He took the children into His arms and embraced and blessed them, undoubtedly the same as He did at another place, one at a time.[142] His ministry was not to the anonymous masses but always to the individual heart. It was against His very soul to turn away one who came seeking Him.

His disciples were to receive little children as if they received Him, and He added this warning: "Whoso shall offend one of these little ones which believe in me, it were better for him that a millstone were hanged about his neck, and that he were drowned in the depth of the sea."[143]

Soon after, a rich young ruler came seeking Him to ask a question. Among the Jews, disciples asked their rabbis searching questions, so it was natural for the young man to ask the Lord, "What shall I do that I may inherit eternal life?"[144] The Savior answered simply, "If thou wilt enter into life, keep the commandments," and then began reciting the Ten Commandments. Yet the rich man wanted more: "All these things have I kept from my youth up: what lack I yet?" Jesus answered, "If thou wilt be perfect, go and sell that thou hast, and give to the poor, and thou shalt have treasure in heaven: and come and follow me." The request tugged at his conscience but was too much, and "he went away sorrowful: for he had great possessions."[145] The issue was not just a matter of heart, the impossibility of serving God and mammon. It is also a question of disparity, the poor all about us who hunger and want, while the rich hoard, live to excess, or exact high prices. The resulting enmity and disparity is not unnoticed by the Lord. An ancient prophet, exhorting his people to pray, added this warning: "If ye turn away the needy, and the naked, . . . your prayer is vain, and availeth you nothing."[146]

Left: Basaltic millstone at Capernaum. The top portion had a wooden handle that protruded and could be attached to work animals to turn the millstone in circles and grind the corn or grain. Average millstones weighed 200 to 500 pounds. The stone is a graphic reminder of the depth of severity the offense of little children is to the Lord.

Above: Light slants across a wall at the entrance to the Church of the Nativity in Bethlehem. Adults who enter here must stoop to pass this 50-inch-high door into this holy site of Christendom. Some think this is a representation of an eye of a needle where camels who would pass through into a city must be unloaded of all burdens and go on their knees to pass. Others take the eye of the needle analogy literally, "but with God all things are possible."[147]

Young mustard flowers growing in a field of mustard twenty miles west of Jerusalem. Mustard is one of the most prolific and abundant plants in all of Israel, further testimony of the Lord's tie of the mustard seed to faith. The Lord's Prayer has a definite Jewish flavor with its longing for the Lord's kingdom to come and for the bread of life, like manna, to be given.

Lord, teach us to pray," Christ's disciples pleaded as they watched Him in communion with His Father. So He taught them a pattern. "Our Father which art in heaven":[148] We are to pray to the Father, the radiant one, "the creator of the shimmering sound that touches us."[149] "Hallowed be thy name": We reverence this Lord above all else. He is more than we can envision, a holy of holies in our hearts. "Thy will be done in earth, as it is in heaven": We long for His kingdom to be established, yearn for the day when He will reign. "Give us this day our daily bread": Still, we live in the mortal here and now, and we look to Him as the giver of every good thing. "And forgive us our sins; for we also forgive everyone who is indebted to us":[150] "Loose the cords of mistakes binding us.

. . . Lighten our load of secret debts as we relieve others of their need to repay."[151] "And suffer us not to be led into temptation, but deliver us from evil":[152] Make us strong and clear. "Don't let surface things delude us."[153] "For thine is the kingdom, and the power, and the glory, for ever. Amen."[154]

130

A question facing humanity throughout the centuries has been "What is most important? How do I spend my time, the energies of my spirit?" Jesus addressed this one day while visiting the Bethany home of His dear friends Mary and Martha. Martha, the meticulous housekeeper concerned over the details of entertaining Jesus, was "cumbered about much serving," while her sister, Mary, sat at Jesus' feet to be taught. Finally, somewhat dismayed at her sister, Martha asked, "Lord, dost thou not care that my sister hath left me to serve alone? Bid her therefore that she help me." Then came the answer of answers for all of us distracted from our spiritual center by a load of care, undue worry, and incidental duties: "Martha, Martha, thou art careful and troubled about many things: but one thing is needful: and Mary hath chosen that good part, which shall not be taken away from her."[155] Amid all else, the expediencies that nip at us, we must turn our face to the Son.

"Thou shalt love thy . . . neighbor as thyself." This was written in the law, but a certain lawyer, hoping to justify himself, asked, "Who is my neighbour?" Jesus answered with one of the greatest stories in literature. It seems a man went down to Jericho and was beaten, stripped, wounded, and left for dead by thieves along the side of the road. The first upon this pathetic scene was a priest who saw him and passed by on the other side.[156] Stripped and wounded, the man was unidentifiable and perhaps even dead. If he was a Gentile, he was unclean; but worse yet, if he was dead, contact with him would defile a priest. A priest, defiled, could not collect, distribute, or eat the tithes, and his family would go without. To this priest, the safe thing to do was to turn his eyes from the scene and pass on the other side.

Next came a Levite, whose rules were somewhat less strict. Still, contact with a corpse, or with one who might die while he rendered aid, would be ritually defiling. Defiled, a Levite could not eat the wave offering or wear his phylacteries. He looked on the broken man in the ditch, and he too chose to pass on the other side. Perhaps he thought this was the right and proper thing to do, a matter of keeping religious vows.

Last to come was a Samaritan. To a Jew he was an outsider, the hated, the heathen, the brazen Samaritan who lived a tainted religion. "He that eats the bread of the Samaritans," the Mishna declares, "is like to one that eats the flesh of swine."[157] If the beaten man were to awake and see it was a Samaritan who helped him, the Samaritan might receive a spit in the eye for his thanks.

Why would Jesus choose as His prime example of charity a Samaritan? Probably because His doctrines were radical, meant to shake the listeners beyond their prejudices to the core of conscience. When the Samaritan saw the wounded, "he had compassion on him," and he poured oil and wine into his wounds and bound them, then set him on his own beast and brought him to an inn. The next day when he left, he paid the host and said, "Take care of him; and whatsoever thou spendest more, when I come again, I will repay thee." Jesus designed the story not to show just the compassion of the Samaritan but also the price he was willing to pay for his service. "Go, and do thou likewise,"[158] said Jesus.

Left: Late afternoon light touches flowers and a section of the road to Jericho. This was a treacherous road from Jerusalem to Jericho, and people going to and from festivals and holy day celebrations would almost always travel in groups to protect against bandits along the way. The parable drew upon a common danger and fear for people who would travel alone on this well-known road.

Above: The serpentine road to Jericho was prolific with overhanging cliffs and hidden gullies where robbers could hide and attack innocent travelers. Twenty or more people could hide in the confines of this view within forty feet of the road just over the brow of the grass as it drops sharply to the stream bed below.

133

Glow of candlelight through the darkness of the tomb of Lazarus at Bethany. Jewish tombs often had two chambers, one for mourning and one for burial. Jesus knew all things concerning the raising of Lazarus, and yet He let all participate in the miracle: "Where have ye laid him?" yet He knew. "Take ye away the stone,"[159] He cried, and yet He could have called angels or used His power to move it.

Mary and Martha sent an urgent message about their brother to Perea where Jesus was teaching: "Lord, behold, he whom thou lovest is sick." When Jesus heard of Lazarus' sickness, He said, "This sickness is not unto death, but for the glory of God,"[160] and He turned and continued His work two more days at Perea with the calm assurance of divinity, knowing that He would arrive in proper time.

After two days, He told the disciples that Lazarus was dead, but He said, "Let us go into Judaea again." This was a dangerous suggestion, prompting Thomas to say, "Let us also go, that we may die with him," for "they feared lest the Jews should take Jesus and put him to death, for as yet they did not understand the power of God."[161]

As Jesus traveled on the road near Bethany, the news came that Lazarus had already lain in the grave four days, and heartbroken Martha, hearing that Jesus was coming, went out sorrowing to meet Him. "Lord," she exclaimed, "if thou hadst been here, my brother had not died." How often during that heavy four days since Lazarus' death Mary and Martha must have discussed this very thing. "If only Jesus had come, if only He had been here." Still, she had no complaining word for Jesus, no murmuring; she just affirmed, "But I know, that even now, whatsoever thou wilt ask of God, God will give it thee.[162]

Jesus answered, "Thy brother shall rise again," which Martha misunderstood, saying, "I know that he shall rise again in the resurrection, at the last day." Jesus explained further, "I am the resurrection, and the life: he that believeth in me, though he were dead, yet shall he live: . . . Believest thou this?" Then Martha affirmed with loving faith, "Yea, Lord: I believe that thou art the Christ, the Son of God, which should come into the world."[163]

Then Martha went quickly to her sister with words every believer would long to hear: "The Master is come, and calleth for thee." Oh, He had come! As Mary left the home, perhaps with couches and chairs tossed over in the Jewish form of mourning, the mourners followed her, thinking she went to the grave to weep. Instead, she came to the Lord and fell at His feet. Jesus asked, "Where have ye laid him?" to which they answered, "Lord, come and see." Then, "Jesus wept,"[164] not apparently because Lazarus had died, for He knew that in moments His friend would rise. He wept, instead, for love and compassion, for the grief that tore the heart of His friends, for the bruises and scars of mortality, for all that hurts.

At the place of burial, Jesus asked the people to roll away the stone from the cave entrance where Lazarus lay. Martha demurred: "Lord, by this time he stinketh: for he hath been dead four days." Jewish belief was that a body began its corruption on the fourth day. But Jesus turned His eyes heavenward and said, "Father, I thank thee that thou hast heard me." Then in a loud voice that must have shaken the listeners to the marrow, He cried, "Lazarus come forth." And "he that was dead came forth, bound hand and foot with graveclothes." "Then from that day forth [the Pharisees] took counsel together for to put [Christ] to death."[165]

The modern entrance to the tomb of Lazarus in Bethany is twenty-four steps above the original chamber. After the great miracle here, the chief priests and Pharisees took council about Jesus, saying, "What do we do? for this man doeth many miracles."[166] They saw His miracle as a threat that would attract Roman attention, and they feared losing their nation. With raging jealousy, from that day on they sought every opportunity to put Him to death.

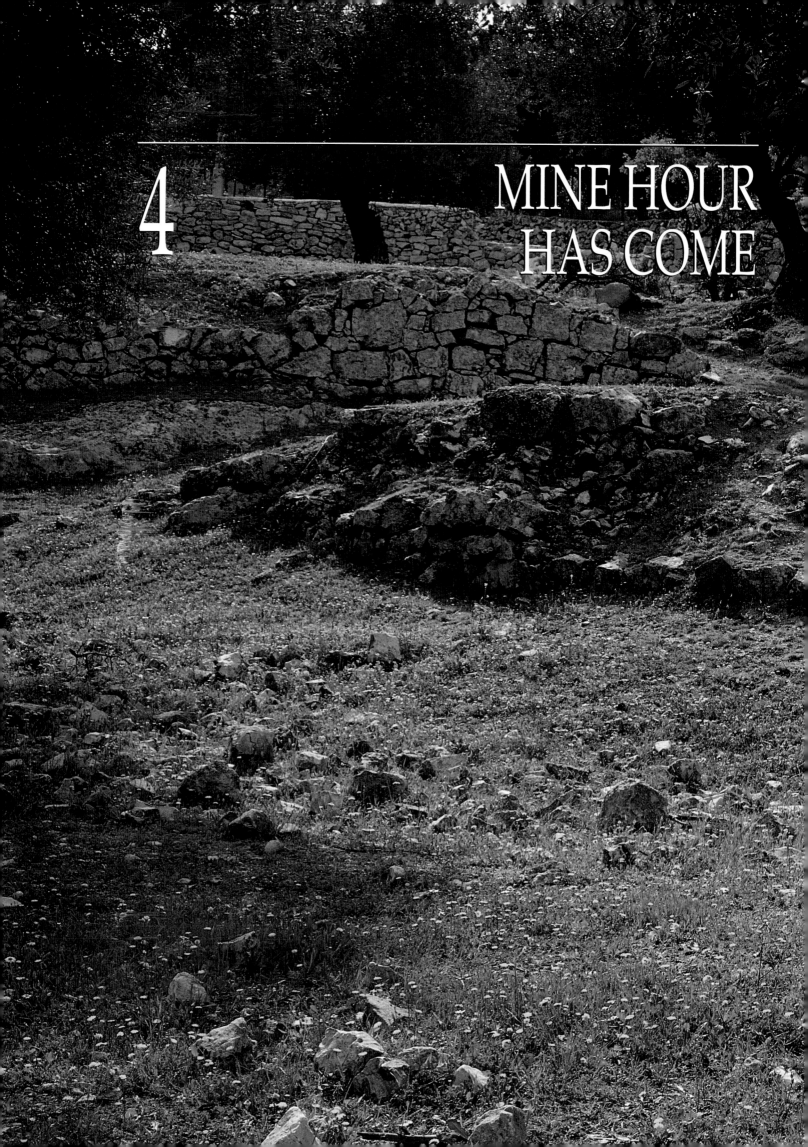

4

MINE HOUR
HAS COME

ow His hour had come. Behind Him were the green hills of Galilee, the great crowds gathering on the grass to hear His word, the lap of waves on a blue sea. Ahead lay Jerusalem, the arrogant city on a hill, tense in its self-conceit, where already in their supreme blindness in the name of religious piety, plotters were scheming to kill the Lord Himself. Offended by His healing touch, by His words that cut to the heart of their hypocrisy, the Roman and Jewish rulers gathered in the high halls of the chief priest and conspired against Him. Jesus' final offense that had challenged their dominion was the raising of Lazarus. "If we let him thus alone, all men will believe on him,"[1] they said. Raising the dead, healing the blind, lifting the broken heart, these were the offenses that kindled their anger and threatened their position.

Still, their fanatical hatred did not stop Jesus from coming to Jerusalem for Passover with the certain knowledge of what He would face. Bitter contempt, insult, and death waited for Him along the shadowed roads of Jerusalem, often from the very people who claimed they represented God. What superb irony! Jesus said, "What shall I say? Father save me from this hour: but for this cause came I unto this hour."[2] In Bethany, just over the hill from Jerusalem, Mary, sister of Martha, anointed His feet with a precious oil that she had saved "against the day of [his] burying,"[3] and He patiently told apostles who could not understand that He would submit Himself to be mocked, scourged, and spat upon. He would overcome the world, but not before it appeared to all those who loved Him that the world had overcome Him. They must face His humiliation before they saw His triumph.

He would suffer that others would not have to suffer, face agonies beyond description to do His Father's will: "For I have not spoken of myself; but the Father which sent me, he gave me a commandment, what I should say, and what I should speak."[4] He had come from His Father, a messenger of love, and, having fulfilled all things, He would return to His Father. His prayer for His closest friends was that they could be one "as thou, Father, art in me, and I in thee, . . . that the world may believe that thou hast sent me."[5]

Pages 136–37: View of an olive vineyard and a garden area on the Mount of Olives a few feet from the traditional site of Gethsemane. The exact place where Jesus suffered is not known today, but the power of the atonement transcends time.

Left: Growing out of seemingly solid rock, two olive trees are joined as one in a Bethlehem vineyard, a symbol of the unity of the Father and the Son. Jesus said, "He that believeth on me, believeth not on me, but on him that sent me. And he that seeth me seeth him that sent me."[6]

Above: Palm leaves are a common protection from the intense rays of the noon sun in the Middle East. As Christ made His triumphal entry, the crowds cut down branches from trees and waved them or twisted them into a matting and strewed them along his path. The waving of palm-branches was the welcome for royalty and kings.

On that Sunday in spring, as Jesus and His band of followers went from Bethany to Jerusalem for the Passover celebration, He instructed two of His disciples to go into a village, where they would find a young colt. On this meek animal He would ride for His triumphal entry into Jerusalem, coming not as a proud king with conquests of war but rather in the rule of peace. The word of His coming had spread among the festive pilgrims gathered in the city, especially among His own Galileans, who had heard of His miracles, and as the fire spread from heart to heart, they rushed out to meet Him, making a rough carpet by unloosing their cloaks and throwing them in His path. Here was the promised Son of David, and now surely the kingdom was at hand! Waving palm leaves, they shouted hosannas: "Blessed be the King that cometh in the name of the Lord."[7] Disgruntled and knowing full well that the people were proclaiming Jesus the Messiah, the Pharisees made a desperate appeal to Him to stop the commotion. He answered that if the people held their peace, the very stones would cry out.

Left: Steep and winding road down the Mount of Olives directly across from the eastern wall of Jerusalem. Leaving Bethany the Sunday before his last Passover, Christ probably came along the ancient caravan road that ran from Jericho to Jerusalem where pilgrims who could not find accommodations in the city were camped. If ever Judah was to have her king, this was the time.

Above: A young colt tied by its mother in Shepherd's Fields near Bethlehem. Christ told his disciples to find "a colt tied whereon never man sat. . . . And if any man say unto you, Why do ye this? say ye that the Lord hath need of him; and straightway he will send him hither."[8] Ancient prophets had seen that the Messiah would make his royal entry on a donkey.

Morning comes to the city of gold, Jerusalem. "Shofar sounding from the temple to call the world to prayer. The shepherd pauses in the valley and peace is every where. How many songs, how many stories, the stony hills recall. Around her heart my city carries a lonely ancient wall. Jerusalem, Jerusalem, Forever young, forever old. My heart will sing your songs of glory. Jerusalem."[9]

As Jesus first caught sight of Jerusalem, that city of palaces and ivory towers, of terraces and magnificent gardens, He wept. Though the multitude cheered as He began His descent down the Mount of Olives, He moaned in deep lamentation. "The contrast was, indeed, terrible between the Jerusalem that rose before Him in all its beauty, glory, and security, and the Jerusalem which He saw in vision . . . with the camp of the enemy around about it on every side."[10] For with God's view, He saw that in A.D. 68, but a few years hence, the Romans would besiege the city until the temple would be left without one stone upon another, until the city would be tumbled to the ground, its former beauty in ashes. Scene after scene must have arisen before His eyes, the gory bodies of Jerusalem's children among her ruins, the famine that drove mothers to snatch food from their infants, the thousands crucified outside the city walls. He said that in those days the daughters of Jerusalem would say,

142

"Blessed are the barren, and the wombs that never bare." "Then shall they . . . say to the mountains, Fall on us; and to the hills, Cover us"[11]—all of this because they had rejected their God.

Because of the threats to His life, Jesus did not stay in Jerusalem but returned each evening of Passover week to Bethany. The next day on His way to the city, He hungered. Seeing a fig tree growing in the rocky soil, He went to pick its fruit but found nothing and cursed it. The fruit of a fig should appear with the leaves, and a tree like this, green and flaunting in its verdancy but absolutely barren, was the perfect symbol of a hypocrite, able to make a good show but to give nothing. "By their fruits ye shall know them,"[12] the Lord had told them, leaving a haunting question by which all can judge their lives: "What are your fruits?" As it was with the fig tree, so it would be with all the self-righteous who make a false show of piety. So it would be with Jerusalem and those who pored over the scriptures but did not know the Lord.

Above: A pigeon flies from a palm-thatched roof in Tiberias near the Sea of Galilee. Pigeons and lambs were among the merchandise sold on the temple grounds. Former high priest Annas owned a temple market called the bazaars of the sons of Annas which stirred popular resentment. When Jesus cleansed the temple, the public was not enraged, but the rulers were indignant at the loss to their income.

Right: Morning light touches the Golden Gate in the eastern city wall as seen from the Kidron Valley. Though hard to document, the story is told that the gate was walled up by the Turks sometime after 1517 to stop the Messiah from entering. Jewish tradition held that the Messiah would enter Jerusalem through that eastern gate. Ironically, Christ had already made his triumphal entry through the eastern gate, one that is directly below the present Golden Gate.

The temple was a place of glory, with solid gold covering the great marble stones of the inner building. But it was also a place of ravenous wolves to the eye of the Lord as He walked through the outer Court of the Gentiles on that Passover week. Vendors haggled over prices on salt, oil, and wine used in the sacrifices, and everywhere the stench and filth of lowing cattle and bleating lambs assaulted the senses of those who came to worship. Money-changers used scales of questionable accuracy for the thriving exchange business of the Roman, Grecian, Egyptian, and Persian coins in common circulation, taking advantage of religious pilgrims. It was a noisy scene of desecration and bloated prices, dishonesty and dispute. As He had done once before at the beginning of His ministry, Jesus boldly went into the temple, overthrowing the tables of the money-changers, their coins scattering across the fouled floor, throwing out the buyers and sellers with indignation. "It is written," He said, "my house is the house of prayer: but ye have made it a den of thieves."[13]

In cleansing the temple, Jesus had upset the money-gouging bazaars of the chief priests and Sanhedrin. Merchants' pockets had been lined by the temple trade, but so had the pockets of some Jewish rulers who were now even more infuriated. On the Monday night of Passover week, just a few hours after the temple cleansing, the chief priests, scribes, and elders consulted together how they might quell the popular acclaim that was attached to this Galilean rebel. For three years they had tried to ensnare Him with devious questions, all to no avail, but now they would raise a new issue. Perhaps they could show that He had no rabbinical authority and therefore no right to teach or even to speak. So, gathering together in all the intimidating power of their age and position, they made their formal challenge, saying, "Tell us, by what authority doest thou these things? or who is he that gave thee this authority?"[14]

Palestine is a land dotted with olive vineyards, the gnarled trees with their dusty leaves lining the rocky hills and valleys. Thus for part of His answer, Jesus told this parable, using images familiar to them all: "A certain man planted a vineyard, and let it forth to husbandmen, and went into a far country for a long time."[15] "And at the season he sent to the husbandmen a servant, that he might receive from the husbandmen of the fruit of the vineyard. And they caught him, and beat him, and sent him away empty." The vineyard owner sent more servants, and the same happened to them; they were beaten, wounded, or killed. Finally, all his messengers having been shamefully treated, the owner sent his well-beloved and only son, saying, "They will reverence my son."[16] But the greedy overseers of the vineyard treated the heir no better, killing him and casting him out of the vineyard.

The analogy was clear. The Lord had planted His people Israel on earth as His vineyard and then returned to heaven, sending His servants the prophets to labor in the vineyard and receive an accounting. But Israel too often had misused, mocked, and killed God's messengers. Now the Lord had sent His own beloved Son, whose fate would be the same. The fruit of the vineyard would be evil and corrupt: "And it came to pass that the Lord of the vineyard wept, and said . . . , What could I have done more for my vineyard?"[17]

Collapsing tower in a vineyard flanked by dead olive trees, decayed with time. A tower was common in well-cared-for vineyards in ancient Israel, where the master or his servants could watch for thieves. Besides fencing his vineyard, gathering out stones, and planting the choicest vine, the Lord specifically states that He "built a tower in the midst of it."[18] Yet after all this care, it brought forth only wild fruit.

147

What shall the Lord do to these husbandmen who had killed His Son in the parable of the vineyard? If these elders and scribes wondered, Jesus had a ready answer, a scathing denunciation: "He will come and destroy these husbandmen, and will give the vineyard unto others."[19]

Who gave Him authority? Not to be trapped, He answered their question with a brilliant question of His own. "The baptism of John, was it from heaven, or of men?" Now it was the elders and scribes who were caught, for if they said, "Of heaven," then they were admitting that John was sent of God, and his witness of Jesus was binding upon them. If, however, they said, "Of earth," the multitude who loved John would rise up against them. They, who were supposed to know scriptural answers, could only mumble a humiliating reply—they could not say.[20]

Denounced, humiliated, caught in their own pretensions, the elders' hatred intensified into an emphatic decision—they would put Him to death. But for fear of an uproar from the people, they must do it with subtlety. At that very moment, a traitor played into their hands, one of the Lord's own Twelve, Judas Iscariot. They did not go to him; out of the darkness of his heart, he came to them. The betrayal was his initiative. Without the tumult of open arrest, he would lead them to the Lord, for, as a friend, he knew the garden where Christ ofttimes resorted for private retreat. But he would do it for a price—thirty pieces of silver, ironically paid to him from the accursed temple treasury.

How could one who had felt the Lord's touch, who had seen the dead raised and the lame walk, be consumed in such utter darkness? How could he turn from those kind eyes to clutch a paltry thirty pieces of silver? Perhaps it was ambition, perhaps greed. Perhaps it was the hope that Jesus would openly declare political deliverance to his followers. For Judas, Jesus was not the bright king of earthly reign who would bring honor and wealth to his followers. Luke says it simply, "Then entered Satan into Judas,"[21] and as he sold his master for the legal price of a slave, he sold his own soul.

It was Thursday of the Lord's final week, and that day He and His apostles would share the Passover, their last supper together. Some confusion has arisen because John wrote that the next day, Friday, as Jesus stood in mortifying trial before Pilate, "it was the preparation of the passover," the day when the Jews would search their houses and destroy anything containing leaven, the day they would take their yearling lambs to the gleaming white and gold temple for sacrifice, bearing them home again on their shoulders for the feast that night. How could the Lord and His apostles have eaten their Passover meal instead on Thursday? Best evidence suggests that the Lord and His apostles, being Galileans, followed a calendar that began at sunrise. Thus 14 Nissan, the day of Passover preparation, began Thursday morning, and their meal was eaten that night. However, on the Judean calendar, 14 Nissan began Thursday at sunset, and the killing of the sacrificial lambs occurred on Friday afternoon before 14 Nissan had ended. Therefore, at that same hour when the bleating of thousands of sacrificial lambs went silent, the Lamb of God, who "was lifted up upon the cross and slain for the sins of the world,"[23] would also cease to breathe. The last symbolic sacrifices were offered at the very moment of the ultimate sacrifice. All things bore record of Christ and His mission for those who had eyes to see.

For their paschal meal, the last supper, the Lord sent Peter and John ahead to make preparations, saying with seeric vision that they were to go into the city where they would meet a man bearing a pitcher of water, an unusual sight in Palestine, where carrying water was women's work. They were to follow him into a house where the master, probably a loving disciple, would have prepared a large upper room, already furnished for the feast.

It may have been just at sunset as Jesus and the other ten apostles descended the Mount of Olives and entered the Holy City in all its festive attire. The evening lamps were lit; the lamb had been roasted on a pomegranate spit; the bitter herbs, the vinegar, the unleavened cakes were ready as Jesus reclined at the table over which He would preside.

Pages 148–49: Aceldama is known as the field of blood purchased with the 30 pieces of silver Judas received for betraying the Lord. When Judas saw that Jesus was condemned, his soul shrieked, "I have betrayed innocent blood," to which the chief priests replied, "What is that to us?" Then, flinging the silver onto the temple floor, he "went and hanged himself." Taking up the silver pieces, the chief priests purchased this field for the burial of strangers.[22]

Right: Innocent, new lamb on the bedrock of the hills of Bethlehem. In Egypt at the first Passover, Israel brushed their doorways with the blood of a lamb so that the destroying angel would pass by. In all the Passovers to follow, they sacrificed an unblemished lamb on the altar. These symbols were to remind them that it is only through the blood of the Lamb of God, His atoning sacrifice, that we can pass through the door into eternal life, escaping spiritual death.

Their mood was somber, their hearts burdened as Jesus and His friends took the several hours to eat the Passover meal and perform its accompanying rituals. "Why is this night different from all others? Why do we eat only unleavened bread, bitter herbs, and roasted lamb?" they would have asked and answered. Whatever the traditional answers, for them this night was different because the Lord would soon leave them, and they bore a love for Him that made the thought unbearable. In just hours, they would look for Him and find Him not. He would say, "Whither I go, ye cannot come." Then, "supper being ended," Jesus arose, "laid aside his garments; and took a towel, and girded himself,"[24] poured water into a basin, and began to wash the disciples' feet. The feet of those in Palestine, clad only in sandals as they trod the filthy streets strewn with dirt and dung, were distasteful by day's end. Washing another's feet was the lowest of jobs, fit only for the utterly servile, fit not just for a servant but for a slave.

Thinking His Master too noble for such a task, Peter demurred, "Thou shalt never wash my feet," to which Jesus answered, "If I wash thee not, thou hast no part with me." Then the impulsive, exuberant Peter, fired with love for the Lord, said, "Lord, not my feet only, but also my hands and my head." As He poured the water over their feet, He wanted the memory borne deeply into conscience. "If I then, your Lord and Master, have washed your feet; ye also ought to wash one another's feet."[25] The greatest was not the one with the most acclaim or honor, doing work of power and distinction, but the quiet servant, meeting the unspoken need.

Then Jesus told them something that shocked their sensibilities: "One of you which eateth with me shall betray me." They all asked sorrowfully, "Is it I?"[26] John, lying on Jesus' breast, asked who it was, and Jesus answered, perhaps to him alone, "He it is, to whom I shall give a sop."[27] Then dipping the sop, He gave it to Judas, who asked with mock dismay, "Master, is it I?" "Thou hast said,"[28] answered Jesus. "That thou doest, do quickly."[29] And Judas hurried out alone into eternal darkness.

"Little children, yet a little while I am with you," said Jesus in that upper room, and as His death approached, love was foremost on His mind. It was love that undergirded His life and His final sacrifice, love that never sought its own, love that didn't waiver before those who were wretchedly unloveable. Now He asked of those who would follow Him, "A new commandment I give unto you, That ye love one another; as I have loved you, that ye also love one another."[30] This love would be a distinguishing mark of their discipleship.

Nothing communicated love more clearly than the Lord's institution of the sacrament: "As they were eating, Jesus took bread and brake it, and blessed it, and gave to his disciples, and said, Take, eat; this is in remembrance of my body which I gave a ransom for you. And he took the cup, and gave thanks, and gave it to them, saying, Drink ye all of it. For this is in remembrance of my blood of the new testament, which is shed for as many as shall believe on my name, for the remission of their sins."[31] The Passover had been a symbolic looking forward to the blood of the Lamb, which would be shed as a ransom for the sins of all those who would believe on His name. The sacrament was in remembrance of Him with a dual pledge that all those who partook would take upon themselves His glorious name and He would send His Spirit to be with them. They could not save themselves from sin and death, but, through His sinless life, He could. For this reason He had come. What inexpressible comfort for these disciples in this awful hour.

Then Jesus, with the absolute knowledge of the events of that night, gave them news to make the heart shudder: "All ye shall be offended because of me this night: for it is written, I will smite the shepherd, and the sheep shall be scattered"—scattered by fear, and the sword, and the trembling of the spirit. Could this be true for every one of His closest friends? But Peter with a rush of heartfelt emotion said, "Although all shall be offended, yet will not I."[32] "I am ready to go with thee, both into prison, and to death," to which Christ sadly replied, "I tell thee, Peter, the cock shall not crow this day, before that thou shalt thrice deny that thou knowest me."[33]

Pages 152–53: The upper room, traditional site of the last supper. The site may be close, but this room actually dates back only to 1335. Some have speculated that the actual upper room may have been in the home of John Mark, who wrote the second Gospel. Judas probably led the soldiers there first and then to Gethsemane with Mark following. Mark may have been the young man seized at the arrest, who, leaving his linen cloth, fled naked, for his is the only Gospel that tells this story.

Left: Light flows through holes in a covered street of Jerusalem. This market runs west from the temple mount where modern traders work as did their ancestors of old.

Above: The hyssop was used by the Israelites as a paintbrush to mark their doorposts with blood. After the first Passover, the hyssop reminded them to remain humble. Tradition has it that on Golgotha the Lord was given vinegar to drink, passed up to him on the branches of the hyssop.

155

P eace" was a greeting given among the Jews. *Shalom.* On this night as the lights began to burn low in the upper room, the Lord offered the deepest peace: "Peace I leave with you, my peace I give unto you: not as the world giveth, give I unto you." When armies clash, when neighbors look at each other with enmity, when the ambitious are relentlessly self-seeking, when fear and worry clutch the soul and cloud all good intentions, when one can never get enough, this is not peace. Peace, in fact, can never be the gift of the world and its inclinations. It is the natural gift of knowing God, of living radically different from the world. Submissive instead of willful, forgiving instead of revengeful, willing to suffer instead of seeing another suffer, loving not just friends but also enemies. With these principles Christ's true followers would be utterly set apart, and He could say to them just minutes before He faced all the torment that Satan could unleash upon Him, "Let not your heart be troubled, neither let it be afraid."[34]

It was a night for Him to reveal hidden mysteries of the king-dom. They would soon be persecuted as the devotees of an executed criminal, and He needed to prepare them. While He was with them, He could comfort and bless them, give them courage when they faltered. And now He promised, "I will not leave you comfortless: I will come to you." If they loved Him and kept His command-ments, He would send them another Comforter that would abide with them forever—"Even the Spirit of truth; . . . for he dwelleth with you, and shall be in you."[35] What extraordinary and powerful comfort this was can be seen in the later lives of those who listened intently to His words. Peter, that very night, would retreat in fear and deny that he knew the Lord, but only days later at Pentecost, when he received the Holy Ghost—this Comforter—he became mighty and unshakable.

Then Thomas, thinking of his Lord's imminent departure, asked, "Lord, we know not whither thou goest." How will we find you when you are gone? Jesus answered, "I am the way, the truth, and the life." "In my Father's house are many mansions. . . . I go to prepare a place for you."[36]

156

Pages 156–57: An eerie, cloud-streaked moon shines over Absalom's Tomb in the Kidron Valley near where Christ and his apostles walked on their way to Gethsemane after the last supper. This picture was taken on the anniversary of the very night, based on the Jewish lunar calendar. Since the tomb was probably already standing in Christ's day, this is likely the scene the Lord would have viewed just before His anguish in the garden.

Above: The Lord and His apostles crossed this brook in the Kidron Valley on their way to Gethsemane that last night of His life. The Kidron is a narrow wadi nearly three miles long lying between Jerusalem and the Mount of Olives. This place would have been walked many times by the Master, since He went to Gethsemane often with His disciples for retreat from the hostility of Jerusalem.

They sang together with the last cup of their Passover meal, sang perhaps in a circle, as if offering a prayer. Then with whispered conversation they came out of the gate of the city, down the steep hill, and through the Kidron Valley, the sound of running water from a swift brook filling the air. Behind them were the oil lights of a celebrating city, ahead just a few hundred feet the dark specter of the Mount of Olives, where olive trees still grow in healthy abundance, the very image He needed for further teaching about their relationship to Him.

"I am the vine," He said, "ye are the branches: He that abideth in me, and I in him, the same bringeth forth much fruit: for without me ye can do nothing."[37] What, nothing? Despite our pretended self-sufficiency, without Christ we are as worthless as a branch broken from a tree, withered, dry, and utterly useless. And who were these eleven without Him "but unschooled Galileans, some of them fishermen, one a publican, the rest of undistinguished attainments, and all of them weak mortals?"[38] Therefore, if, like us all, they were wandering, unsure, and helpless without Him, He implored, "Ask." "If ye abide in me, and my words abide in you, ye shall ask what ye will, and it shall be done unto you."[39] Again, "Whatsoever ye shall ask the Father in my name, he will give it you."[40]

Ask the Father in my name. "For the Father himself loveth you, because ye have loved me."[41] For them as for us all, He would be their intercessor with the Father, plead their cause, advocate their case. Because they had believed on Him, and therefore on the Father who had sent Him, He would no longer call them His servants but His friends. "I have loved you," He said. "I have loved you."[42]

Then He explained what He would do because of this love. He would give His very life: "Greater love hath no man than this, that a man lay down his life for his friends."[43] For their love for Him they would weep and lament in the next days, weep while the world rejoiced, but He who has the power to promise said, "Your sorrow shall be turned into joy. A woman when she is in travail hath sorrow, because her hour is come: but as soon as she is delivered of the child, she remembereth no more the anguish, for joy that a man is born into the world."[44]

Still, discipleship for them would not be without its terrible costs. The world would hate them as it had hated Him. They would be excommunicated, turned out of the synagogues, and become social outcasts. He said, "Whosoever killeth you will think that he doeth God service. And these things will they do unto you, because they have not known the Father, nor me." He told them of this shadowed future not to dismay or unnerve them, not to make them shiver in the night, but to strengthen them, that when these things "shall come, ye may remember that I told you of them."[45]

Then Jesus lifted up His eyes to heaven to pray, pleading with His Father not for Himself but for His loyal followers who would in the next cruel hours lose His sustaining presence. "I pray for them . . . which thou hast given me. . . . I pray not that thou shouldest take them out of the world, but that thou shouldest keep them from the evil."[46] In that long night and the years to come, they would need this prayer.

They crossed the Kidron brook, the light of a nearly full moon illuminating the way, and climbed the Mount of Olives to the Garden of Gethsemane, a place where they had often retreated together. This garden was actually an olive vineyard, its name *Gethsemane* meaning "place of the olive press," and in this hour there would be inconceivable, heartrending pressing for the Lord. Taking only Peter, James, and John beyond the garden entrance, He "began to be sore amazed, and to be very heavy,"[57] saying to them, "My soul is exceeding sorrowful, even unto death: tarry ye here, and watch with me." Then removing Himself about a stone's throw, in the depths of anguish He "fell on his face, and prayed, saying, O my Father, if it be possible, let this cup pass from me,"[48] "nevertheless not my will, but thine be done."[49] "Abba,"[50] He called, using the intimate personal word for "Father" used particularly in family circles.

The intense agony Jesus faced in the garden was not from fear of death or the pain of crucifixion. As the Son of an eternal Father, no one could take His life from Him. But in these midnight hours He would face the ultimate contest with all the powers of darkness as He took upon Himself the pain, sin, infirmities, and anguish of a corrupted world. "It was not physical pain, nor mental anguish alone, that caused Him to suffer such torture as to produce an extrusion of blood from every pore; but a spiritual agony of soul such as only God was capable of experiencing. No other man, however great his powers of physical or mental endurance, could have suffered so; for his human organism would have succumbed, and . . . produced unconsciousness and welcome oblivion. In that hour of anguish, Christ met and overcame all the horrors that Satan, 'the prince of this world' could inflict."[51]

In modern revelation, Jesus says of the event, "I, God, have suffered these things for all, that they might not suffer if they would repent; but if they would not repent, they must suffer even as I; which suffering caused myself, even God, the greatest of all, to tremble because of pain, and to bleed at every pore, and to suffer both body and spirit—and would that I might not drink the bitter cup and shrink."[52]

An olive press in ancient Israel was used to crush the bitter olives under mighty pressure until they yielded sweet oil for light and healing. So was the Lord crushed under mighty pressure for the same reason. "Is any sick among you?" asked James. "Let him call for the elders of the church; and let them pray over him, anointing him with oil in the name of the Lord."[53] This same oil, used in the healing of the sick, anoints with symbolic power from Gethsemane.

161

Some of the olive trees still standing in the traditional Garden of Gethsemane on the Mount of Olives are at least 1,800 years old and may have been silent witnesses to the Lord's agony. "God so loved the world that he gave his only begotten Son, that whosoever believeth in him should not perish, but have everlasting life."[54] Tradition says that the angel who appeared to strengthen Jesus in the garden was, appropriately, Michael, who, as Adam, had brought about the fall.

In complete anguish of body and spirit, Christ endured the unendurable, "and his sweat was as it were great drops of blood falling down to the ground." "There appeared an angel unto him from heaven, strengthening him. And being in an agony, he prayed more earnestly."[55] This obedient Son whose communication with His Father was so perfect that He could say, "He that hath seen me hath seen the Father,"[56] prayed yet more earnestly. What words He must have said in that impassioned prayer, as He in some way incomprehensible to mortal minds took upon Himself the punishment for all the sins of the world, however loathsome, paying the price, the incalculable debt for our weaknesses that we could not pay. He paid the price, with an infinite atonement, for all who would repent in His name and be at one again with the Lord. Since all things past, present, and future are continually before the Lord,[57] in some way we cannot understand, even the sins we will yet commit added to the agony Christ faced in Gethsemane.

Without this bitter cup, the drinking of whose dregs was the weightiest task in all the universe, we would be spiritually dead. Once having sinned, we would be unclean, unable to return to our Heavenly Father, debtors faced with an impossible debt. Without repentance, the day will come when with absolute clarity we will stand before the bar of God and "shall have a perfect knowledge of all our guilt, and our uncleanness, and our nakedness."[58] With repentance, made possible by a perfect Son, a sacrificial Lamb, paying a price that was not His, our staggering burdens of sin and guilt can be lifted, and we can be given new life. Who in this heartbreaking world of self-disappointment does not need this gift? When in the sorrow of our hearts we cry out, "O Jesus, thou Son of God, have mercy on me, who am in the gall of bitterness,"[59] there is One who hears with mercy because of this night in Gethsemane.

One who saw this scene in vision records, "I seemed to be in the Garden of Gethsemane, a witness of the Savior's agony. I saw Him as plainly as ever I have seen anyone. Standing behind a tree in the foreground, I beheld Jesus, with Peter, James and John, as they came through a little wicket gate at my right. . . . As He prayed

the tears streamed down his face, which was toward me. I was so moved at the sight that I also wept, out of pure sympathy. My whole heart went out to him: I loved him with all my soul, and longed to be with him as I longed for nothing else. . . . The Savior, with the three Apostles, . . . were about to depart. . . . I could endure it no longer. I ran from behind the tree, fell at his feet, clasped Him around the knees, and begged him to take me with him. I shall never forget the kind and gentle manner in which He stooped, raised me up, and embraced me. . . . I felt the very warmth of his body, as he held me in his arms and said in tenderest tones: 'No, my son, these have finished their work; they can go with me; but you must stay and finish yours.' Still I clung to him. Gazing up into his face—for he was taller than I—I besought him fervently: 'Well, promise me that I will come to you at the last.' Smiling sweetly, He said, 'That will depend entirely upon yourself.'"[60]

Trunk of this ancient olive tree in the Garden of Gethsemane seems to be twisted in pain in memory of what happened here. "I stand all amazed at the love Jesus offers me, Confused at the grace that so fully he proffers me. I tremble to know that for me he was crucified, That for me, a sinner, he suffered, he bled and died. Oh, it is wonderful that he should care for me enough to die for me! Oh, it is wonderful, wonderful to me!"[61]

Pages 164–65: The oil from olive trees like this one in the Garden of Gethsemane was ancient Israel's source of light. Without the glow from oil lamps, at night Israel would have been swallowed up in darkness. Christ's atonement in the garden keeps all of humanity from being swallowed in darkness. "The light shineth in darkness; and the darkness comprehendeth it not."[62] *"Comprehendeth" means that the darkness cannot overcome or extinguish the light.*

As all things were created to bear record of the Savior, so Gethsemane, the oil press, bears silent testimony of that grueling night. Olive oil was the very essence of life for Israel. Light came in a dark night because olive oil filled the lamps. Balm and healing came because olive oil was poured into wounds. Olive mash was fuel. But olive oil was obtained from the olives only by subjecting them to extraordinary pressure, crushing them under a stone press. Under this relentless weight, the olive, which is bitter, produced oil, which is sweet. So it is with the atonement. From the bitterness of that night came all that is precious and sweet about life, all that gives light in the the darkness. When we are anointed with consecrated oil, it is through Christ's sacrifice that we are healed, given balm from the olive press He faced for our wounds.

He had asked His apostles Peter, James, and John to watch with Him, but twice when He arose from prayer He found them "sleeping for sorrow."[63] Jesus said, "What, could ye not watch with me one hour?" Then He added in sympathy, "The spirit indeed is willing, but the flesh is weak."[64] Finally, the third time He came and found them asleep, He said, "Sleep on now, and take your rest: it is enough; . . . behold, the Son of man is betrayed into the hands of sinners."[65]

Perhaps even at that minute He could already see the string of torchlights coming up the mount, a multitude of armed soldiers led by Judas. "Mine own familiar friend, in whom I trusted, which did eat of my bread, hath lifted up his heel against me."[66] Approaching Jesus, Judas greeted Him and "not only kissed [him], but covered Him with kisses, kissed Him repeatedly, loudly, effusively."[67] Defending Jesus against the arrest, Peter raised his sword and cut off the right ear of Malchus, the high priest's servant. Touching the ear, Jesus healed it, saying, "Thinkest thou that I cannot now pray to my Father, and he shall presently give me more than twelve legions of angels?"[68] But now was the time for divine restraint as He allowed Himself to be taken captive that the scriptures might be fulfilled.

As the soldiers took Jesus, "they saw before them nothing but a weary unarmed man, whom one of His own most intimate followers had betrayed, and whose arrest was simply watched in helpless agony by a few terrified Galileans"[69] who finally fled in panic. This was the beginning of a long and terrible night of inquisition. First, He was led to degenerate Annas, the former High Priest for seven years, the money-hungry usurper of Jewish power. One of the abominable men of the earth, He appointed and controlled the High Priest, who would have slavishly followed his word.

Next, in exhaustion, He was led bound to Caiaphas, the legal High Priest in whose palace at least a quorum of the Sanhedrin was gathered. They had before them a prisoner innocent of any crime. "Their dilemma was real, for they themselves were sharply divided on all major issues save one—that the man Jesus must die."[70] However, since they needed to find a charge, they sought false witnesses. Many were eager to bare false witness, but "their testimony was *so* false, so shadowy, so self-contradictory, that it all melted to nothing."[71] Through all their hopeless argument, Jesus listened in majestic silence, which only confounded them more until Caiaphas, enraged, hurled this question: "Answerest thou nothing? . . . I adjure thee by the living God, that thou tell us whether thou be the Christ, the Son of God." Jesus answered, for it had never been a secret, "Thou hast said."[72]

Meanwhile, Peter waited in the courtyard below, mingling with the crowd and listening to malcontents tell stories of the arrest. The damsel who had admitted him to the palace said, "Art not thou also one of this man's disciples?" "I am not,"[73] he said. Later another maid said, "This fellow was also with Jesus of Nazareth." This time Peter, more threatened, denied with an oath, saying, "I do not know the man."[74] Then later as Peter was warming himself by the fire, another said, "Surely thou art one of them,"[75] and "Did not I see thee in the garden with him?"[76] Peter cursed and swore with an oath, "Man, I know not what thou sayest."[77] Just then the cock crew, and the Lord, probably being led out a suffering prisoner, turned and looked upon Peter. Seeing that face of love, those suffering eyes, and knowing his own desperation, Peter went out and wept bitterly.

Left: Ancient stone steps dating back to the time of Christ. They lead to the possible site of Caiaphas' palace. These are likely the stone steps Christ climbed on his way to a night of brutal interrogation. In reality, once Annas had decided that Christ should be murdered, the other trials were but a sham.

Above: Ancient flagstones that were once a part of a paved square in the Antonia Fortress where Christ came before Pilate. Games once played by idle Roman soldiers are still seen scratched into the surface. The soldiers never played a crueler sport than when they tortured the Lord. "All they that see me laugh me to scorn."[78]

After the Savior's interview with Caiaphas, Christ's captors spit in His face and buffeted Him and made up a cruel game. Blindfolding Him, they slapped Him with the palms of their hands and then taunted, "Prophesy, who is it that smote thee?" When, at last, the lingering hours of the night had passed, Jesus was brought before the Sanhedrin for the sham of a trial, which would be in flagrant violation of their own laws. The charge was blasphemy against the only one who could not commit blasphemy—the Lord Himself. "What need we any further witness?"[79]

They were, however, bent on His death, and being subject to Roman overlords, they could not impose it themselves. So, followed by a riotous mob, they led Him bound to Herod's magnificent palace, where Pilate, the Roman procurator, was keeping a wary watch over the Passover rabble. This being a Gentile house with leavened bread, the fastidious Jewish leaders would not defile themselves and enter, though ironically they found no defilement in seeking to kill the innocent. Thus it was that Pilate came out to them, asking, "What accusation bring ye against this man?" It was a hard question from a practical politician, and they had searched for and found the charge— not blasphemy, which would mean nothing to a Roman. No, this time they charged Him with sedition. He is a traitor to Caesar. He calls Himself the king of the Jews! Of all those who examined Jesus, Pilate was the least guilty of malice toward Him. Something about the Lord touched the man, and after questioning Him he said frankly, "I find in him no fault at all."[80] To this the chief priests responded in a clamor of accusations, among which a single word stood out: "Galilee." Pilate thought he saw a way out. With relief, he sent the Savior on to Herod, whose jurisdiction included the green hills of Galilee.

Herod had killed John the Baptist, so before the cruel and insolent questioning of this despot, Jesus said not a word. For the weak, the sick, the child, the sinner, Christ had soothing, loving tones, but for the tyrant He had only silence, all the more infuriating to Herod, for he had longed to see a miracle performed.

Pages 168–69: Jerusalem appears to be smoking with destruction as pillars of clouds climb over the eastern city wall. Against his own impressions Pilate willfully chose to send an innocent man to death. How well Isaiah described the Lord: "He is despised and rejected of men; a man of sorrows, and acquainted with grief: and we hid as it were our faces from him."[81]

Above: Replica at Caesarea of a stone bearing an inscription of the names of Emperor Tiberius and Pontius Pilate. This is the only archaeological evidence ever found of Pilate's existence. Though he normally lived in Caesarea, he came to Jerusalem to help control the political passions easily inflamed during Passover. It is said that his life ended in suicide.

The chief priests and rulers of the people were assembled, and the mocked, spat-upon, exhausted Jesus was once again brought before Pilate. Word of His arrest had spread through the streets of the city, and a mob of onlookers had gathered. To these Pilate made his pronouncement: "Ye have brought this man unto me, as one that perverteth the people: and behold, I, having examined him before you, have found no fault in this man."[82] This could have been enough; the Roman leader had spoken. But the pack of fanatics before him thirsted for blood. Pilate's pity for the Lord was crushed under his cowardice, for Pilate had that most inconvenient of burdens, a guilty past. Several times before, he had ignited Jewish fury against Him. One time, for instance, he had confiscated money from the sacred treasury to build an aqueduct and then had sent soldiers in Jewish costume among the people carrying hidden daggers to punish those who had opposed him. Now he was caught; for past sin, he would sin again, violating his own best instincts.

So he tried another kind of appeasement. It was the custom at Passover to release a criminal. Here were two men, perhaps even standing before the mob as Pilate spoke. One was Barabbas, the leader of an insurrection, a murderer. The other was Jesus, the proclaimer of peace, who raised the dead. "Whom will ye that I release unto you? Barabbas, or Jesus which is called Christ?"[83] Some in that crowd had been healed by the Lord, some had heard His healing words, but the chief priests moved among the people stirring them up until they shouted, "Barabbas. Release Barabbas."

Pilate would have released Jesus, and his feelings were even more stirred when his wife came to him pleading, "Have thou nothing to do with that just man: for I have suffered many things this day in a dream because of him."[84] Whatever these flickerings of conscience, Pilate sent Jesus to be scourged. The soldiers wove a crown of thorns and jammed it on that tired head; they placed a purple robe on His shoulders and then, gloating and leering, they smote Him and spit upon Him, saying, "Hail, king of the Jews!"[85] Consider this humiliation, this stinging injustice, and know that He who has suffered all things can succor us in every hour.

Now Pilate brought the bleeding, wounded Jesus again before the crowd. "Behold the man!" he said. Was there even now no

stirrings of pity for Him? Where was the man or woman who would speak up? Where were all those who were waving palms just five days before? Their hosannas had vanished on a fickle wind. No, there was only Pilate's corrupt voice repeating, "I find no fault in Him." It was still early morning when Pilate gave in: "Shall I crucify your King?" and the people answered, "Away with him, crucify him. . . . We have no king but Caesar."[86]

"When Pilate saw that he could prevail nothing, but that rather a tumult was made, he took water, and washed his hands before the multitude, saying, I am innocent of the blood of this just person." And the people shouted, "His blood be on us, and on our children."[87] So Jesus, numbered with the transgressors, carried His cross to the place of the skull, Golgotha, until He collapsed under the weight and mounting misery. The men along the road were silent; some women wept. The cross was raised between two thieves, and at noon the earth turned dark in shame.

The Lord was crucified outside the city wall at Golgotha, meaning "place of a skull." This rock, with its curves and caves much resembling a skull, has been suggested as the possible site. Though Christ's crucifixion has been painted as if it were on a hill, Roman tradition was to crucify along the road that all passersby might see, adding to the victim's humiliation.

Pages 172–73: Darkening purple sky backdrops an unusual tree at Golgotha. After Christ had died, the soldiers pierced his side with a sword, and water gushed forth. "And when I think that God, his Son not sparing, Sent him to die, I scarce can take it in, That on the cross my burden gladly bearing He bled and died to take away my sin. Then sings my soul, my Savior God, to thee, How great thou art! How great thou art!"[88]

For capital punishment, the Jews stoned, burned, beheaded, or strangled, but the Romans chose the cruelest punishment of all—crucifixion. It was a lingering death for its tortured victims. "The unnatural position made every movement painful; the lacerated veins and crushed tendons throbbed with incessant anguish; the wounds, inflamed by exposure, gradually gangrened; . . . there was added to them the intolerable pang of a burning and raging thirst,"[89] dizziness, cramp, starvation, sleeplessness, and shame. In Jerusalem, a charitable women's group administered a mixture of wine and drugs to dull the pain as the victim was stretched on the ground and nailed to the crossbeam, but this Jesus refused.

Stripped, He was raised on the cross with a mocking sign over His head: "JESUS OF NAZARETH THE KING OF THE JEWS."[90] As the soldiers beneath Him cast lots for what was probably His only material possession, a coat without seam, He asked in their behalf, "Father, forgive them; for they know not what they do." As He hung in anguish, the rulers and people gaped and cursed and condemned Him, taunting, "He saved others; let him save himself."[91] Through the anguish, He had only loving words. To His mother, Mary, who must have felt the pangs of near-death in her own body, it was concern that she be cared for. To the beloved John He said, "Behold thy mother,"[92] and from that hour John took her into his own home. To the thief who would repent, He gave hope. At noon the heavens grew black for three hours, as if the universe itself were weeping for the agony of the Creator. In that time all the infinite agonies and merciless pains of Gethsemane returned, and His Father's spirit itself withdrew that the victory might be His. At the ninth hour, 3:00 P.M., "Jesus cried with a loud voice, saying, . . . My God, my God, why hast thou forsaken me?"[93] In that eerie midafternoon darkness, someone ran and filled a sponge with vinegar. Having received the vinegar, Jesus said, "Father, it is finished, thy will is done."[94] As He died, the veil of the temple was rent, and the earth quaked and rocks were rent as if to say with a nearby centurion, "Truly this man was the Son of God."[95]

Through an arched tree like a gate, steps ascend toward the light at Banias near the headwaters of the Jordan. Christ's visit to the spirit world opened the gate for those who died in their sins without a knowledge of the truth or rejected the prophets. In one early source Christ tells the Twelve, "I have received all authority from my Father, so that I might lead out into light those who sit in darkness. You shall become fellow-heirs with me."[96]

While His body yet hung from the cross and then was placed in the tomb of Joseph of Arimathea, Jesus' immortal spirit performed a mission of utmost importance to the plan of salvation. An early Christian asked Peter, "Shall those be wholly deprived of the kingdom of heaven who died before Christ's coming?"[97] Or in any generation, shall those who died without knowledge of the gospel of Jesus Christ be cast out? It is a question that haunts Christian writing and was answered by Christ's visiting the spirit world while His body was entombed.

In the world of spirits were gathered an innumerable host of those who had departed this life, "who had been faithful in the testimony of Jesus while they lived in mortality" and were awaiting His coming to open the gates that bound them. And "they were filled with joy and gladness, and were rejoicing together because the day of their deliverance was at hand." While these spirits were waiting, "the Son of God appeared, declaring liberty to the captives who had been faithful; and there he preached to them the everlasting gospel, the doctrine of the resurrection and the redemption of mankind from the fall, and from individual sins on conditions of repentance." All "bowed the knee and acknowledged the Son of God as their Redeemer and Deliverer from death and the chains of hell. Their countenances shone, and the radiance from the presence of the Lord rested upon them."[98] For those faithful, who had been for so long without their bodies, they would soon follow the Lord to resurrection as "the graves were opened; and many bodies of the saints which slept arose."[99]

But "the Lord went not in person among the wicked and disobedient" while among the spirits, "but behold, from among the righteous, he organized his forces and appointed messengers, clothed with power and authority, and commissioned them to go forth and carry the light of the gospel to them that were in darkness, even to all the spirits of men; and thus was the gospel preached to the dead."[100] Since baptism was a necessary step to enter the kingdom, the early Christians had been taught to baptize for the dead by proxy. Paul understood this doctrine: "Else what shall they do which are baptized for the dead, if the dead rise not at all?"[101]

While it was yet dark on the morning of Sunday after the crucifixion, Mary Magdalene and other women arrived at the tomb of Jesus to mourn and anoint with spices the hastily entombed body. To their utter surprise and sadness, when they looked in the tomb Jesus' body was not there. Mary immediately ran to tell Peter and John of their findings: "They have taken away the Lord out of the sepulchre, and we know not where they have laid him." This news caused the disciples to run speedily to the tomb to see for themselves, "for as yet they knew not the scripture, that he must rise again from the dead." As they looked in the tomb, something in John leaped with joy, and he "believed."[102] Yet he and Peter returned to their residences. As Mary and other women lingered by the tomb, "behold, two men stood by them in shining garments," and "they said unto them, Why seek ye the living among the dead?"[103] "Fear not ye; for we know that ye seek Jesus who was crucified. He is not here; for he is risen, as he said. Come, see the place where the Lord lay."[104]

Left: First light of morning touches the edge of the sepulchre in the Garden Tomb and the track where the large stone was rolled to seal it. On Friday, Christ's body had been hastily taken from the cross and placed in the tomb because the Jewish Sabbath began at sundown. The entrance was sealed and guards watched until an angel "with a countenance . . . like lightning" rolled back the stone, "and for fear of him the keepers . . . became as dead men."[105] Later these guards would be bribed to say Christ's disciples had stolen the body.

Above: Golden interior of the empty Garden Tomb, symbol of all the graves that will one day be empty because of the Lord's free gift of resurrection. "I know that my Redeemer lives. What comfort this sweet sentence gives! He lives, he lives, who once was dead. He lives, my everliving Head. He lives to bless me with his love. He lives to plead for me above."[106]

Above: Though the Garden Tomb has not been verified as the actual site of the Lord's burial, it meets all of the scriptural qualifications. The site must be outside of the city wall; it must have anciently been near a garden; it must have had a large, heavy stone to seal the entrance with a track to roll in; it must be large enough to walk into; it must be near a place of execution. The Garden Tomb meets all these qualifications.

Right: Light spills over ancient steps in the Garden Tomb. It may have been somewhere near this place that Jesus and Mary met. So great and wondrous was the coming forth of the Lord from the tomb that the day was marked and overshadowed the celebration of creation's rest. After the resurrection, the holy Sabbath was changed from the seventh day of the week, Saturday, to the first day of the week, Sunday, and was specifically called the Lord's Day.

As yet, Mary Magdalene did not understand the words of the angels, for her sorrow at the loss of her beloved Lord was so stinging. Mary turned herself away from the tomb and saw someone in the garden whom she did not recognize. He asked her, "Woman, why weepest thou? whom seekest thou?" Supposing Him to be the gardener, she boldly said, "Sir, if thou have borne him hence, tell me where thou hast laid him, and I will take him away." Mary's love for the Lord was so powerful that she offered to physically take the body by herself and see to its proper burial. Now came one of the greatest moments in all of history, for this man was not the gardener—it was Jesus Christ with a resurrected body of flesh and bone. And He made Himself known by simply calling her by name in tones so familiar: "Mary." Now she saw, becoming the first witness of the risen Lord. Her tears of sorrow turned to joy as she exclaimed, "Rabboni,"[107] which means "My beloved master."

What joy to this woman and to all of humanity! "But now is Christ risen from the dead, and become the firstfruits of them that slept. . . . For as in Adam all die, even so in Christ shall all be made alive."[108] Mary Magdalene reached forward to worship and love the Lord. Jesus said to her, "Hold me not; for I am not yet ascended to my Father."[109] Whether this meant for her not to keep Him long or whether she was not to physically touch the Lord is unknown. Perhaps the Lord was reserving His first embrace as a glorified and perfected being for His own Father in Heaven, also a glorified and perfected being.

When Mary told the apostles that she had seen the living Lord, her "words seemed to them as idle tales, and they believed them not."[110] Later Jesus appeared to Peter, His chief apostle, who perhaps may have wondered that the Master would ever again call him His servant. This was a day never to be forgotten. Ancient witnesses declare its truth in the holy records, and witnesses today have it borne to their souls by the power of the Holy Ghost: "He is risen! He is risen! Tell it out with joyful voice. He has burst his three days' prison; Let the whole wide earth rejoice. Death is conquered, man is free. Christ has won the victory."[111]

An empty tomb in a garden reminds us that the Lord lives today with a resurrected, glorified body, and the same promise is offered to all. Resurrection is His free gift. "O death, where is thy sting? O grave, where is thy victory?"[112] "Come," he invites everyone who thirsts, "come ye to the waters; and he that hath no money, come buy and eat; yea, come buy wine and milk without money and without price."[113]

On that same day of resurrection, two of the disciples set out from Jerusalem to Emmaus, some five miles distant. Only one topic coursed between their heavy hearts: their hopes for a mighty Messianic reign now dimmed by their Master's death. In that late afternoon, another wayfarer joined them, Jesus Christ, "but their eyes were holden that they should not know him." He asked them plainly why they were so sad. One of them, Cleopas, answered, "Art thou only a stranger in Jerusalem, and hast not known the things which are come to pass there in these days?" Jesus continued to query, "What things?" "And they said unto him, Concerning Jesus of Nazareth, . . . and how the chief priests and our rulers delivered him to be condemned to death, and have crucified him." Jesus then began to teach them quietly and powerfully: "Ought not Christ to have suffered these things? . . . And beginning at Moses and all the prophets, he expounded unto them in all the scriptures the things concerning himself." Arriving at the village, they pleaded: "Abide with us, for it is toward evening, and the day is far spent." As He dined at their table, He blessed the bread "and brake, and gave to them." Perhaps there was something in His tender voice, or perhaps in the manner of blessing the bread, but in a moment "their eyes were opened, and they knew him; and he vanished out of their sight." "Did not our heart burn within us, while he talked with us by the way, and while he opened to us the scriptures?"[114] they recounted. Shouldn't we have known?

Now these two hurried to Jerusalem and found the eleven apostles meeting behind closed doors, for fear of the Jews, and brought their glad tidings to them. "And as they thus spake, Jesus himself stood in the midst of them, and saith unto them, Peace be unto you." As they gazed upon the Lord, they were terrified, supposing Him to be a spirit. But He calmed them: "Behold my hands and my feet, that it is I myself: handle me, and see; for a spirit hath not flesh and bones, as ye see me have." The disciples yet "believed not for joy, and wondered," but to further show them His corporeal nature, "he said unto them, Have ye here any meat?"[115] And they brought Him some food, which He ate before them all.

Winding road through a pine forest on hills outside of Jerusalem leads to Moza, one of the possible candidates for the ancient village of Emmaus. As they walked with the Lord, the two disciples did not recognize Him. "Then in a moment to my view The stranger started from disguise. The tokens in his hands I knew; the Savior stood before mine eyes.[116]

5

THEN SHALL THEY KNOW THAT I AM THE LORD

The apostles went home to Galilee, to the sea they knew, as they waited for the Lord to come to them again. As seven of them gathered together one day, Peter said, "I go a fishing," to which the others answered, "We also go with thee." They fished through the long hours of the night, hoping to feed their families, but they caught nothing. Undoubtedly bone-weary, their nets empty for their effort, they approached the shore. In the dim light of early morning, they did not recognize Jesus as He called to them, "Children, have ye any meat?" When they answered, "No," He said, "Cast the net on the right side of the ship, and ye shall find." When they did, they were not able to draw the net up for the multitude of fishes. This abundant giving was an immediate sign to John. "It is the Lord,"[2] he said. Who else gives like this?

Impulsive Peter put on his fisher's coat and scrambled into the water while the others followed in the ship, dragging the net of fishes. On shore, the Lord, always meeting the smallest need, had prepared a fire of coals where fish were broiling for the hungry men. "Come and dine," He said. After they had eaten, Jesus asked Peter a question that must have wrung his very heart: "Lovest thou me more than these?"—more than the fish, more than the fear of men, more than life itself? Did Peter remember his three denials as he answered, his broken promise that he would never be offended because of the Lord? "Yea, Lord: thou knowest that I love thee." Then Christ said, "Feed my lambs." Then a second time, "Lovest thou me?" and Peter answered again, "Yea, Lord; thou knowest that I love thee." And Christ said, "Feed my sheep." A third time the question was repeated, and "Peter was grieved because he said unto him the third time, Lovest thou me?"[3]

He must have wondered if the Lord distrusted him. Yet this repeated question showed the utmost sensitivity from the Lord. Peter bore three wounds in his heart from his cowardly denials of the Lord. Now he was able to affirm three times that he loved the Lord, each proclamation of devotion a healing for his soul. He would now wear out his life in spreading the Lord's gospel and finally follow his master to crucifixion.

Pages 184–85: Clouds gather over the Jezreel Valley, where in a day to come soldiers will clash. Armageddon *is a Greek transliteration of the Hebrew* Har Megiddon, *"Mountain of Megiddo." Megiddo is an ancient city that stood at the strategic head of the valley and was the scene of several violent and crucial battles in ancient times. It will yet be the place of the most decisive war in the history of the earth.*

Right: Sunrise touching the waters at the north shore of the Galilee near Capernaum. The multitude of great fishes that the apostles brought in at this shore likely weighed between one and three tons. The Lord's tender care for His flock is so evident in his caring for Peter. The Lord said to him, "Satan hath desired to have you, that he may sift you as wheat: but I have prayed for thee, that thy faith fail not." Then the Lord gave Peter the pattern for all of us: "And when thou art converted, strengthen thy brethren."[1]

Sunset washes light over the mountains to the west of Mt. Arbel in the Galilee. Jesus repeatedly reminded the disciples that after the resurrection he would meet them in the Galilee. Surely word spread quickly after the risen Lord had been seen that there would be a meeting in the Galilee. Paul records that "he was seen of above five hundred brethren at once,"[4] not counting women and children, and likely this refers to that special meeting.

The gospels give us only the merest hint of the appearances of the Risen Lord to His beloved followers, only the merest taste of His teachings during the forty-day ministry immediately following the resurrection. Perhaps they were too deep to share, for John tells us, "Many other signs truly did Jesus in the presence of his disciples, which are not written in this book."[5] It was a higher and holier teaching given to those who had proved themselves worthy. Early Christian records describe it as secret, the last and highest revelation, a knowledge given only to those who ask for it, accompanied by specific rites and ordinances.[6] The apostles who had been fearful and vacillating before the Lord's death went forth after these forty days bold and mighty in knowledge and testimony.

One of the Lord's most significant appearances during this time was to a group of at least five hundred men and an uncounted number of women and children on a mountain in Galilee. The instructions given there clearly burst old boundaries. No longer was the

gospel to be preached only to the Jew, only to the house of Israel. Now the mission was sweeping: "Go ye . . . and teach all nations."[7]

The direction was echoed on that final day on the Mount of Olives when, in His last words to the apostles, the Lord instructed, "Ye shall be witnesses . . . unto the uttermost part of the earth."[8] Then He was taken up, and a cloud received Him out of their sight.

Soon after, as promised, He went to "other sheep . . . which are not of this fold: them also I must bring, and they shall hear my voice."[9] These were the Nephites, a branch of the house of Israel, who had left Jerusalem in 600 B.C. and settled in the Americas, a people whose prophets had told them of the Lord's coming and had yearned for the day. Clothed in a white robe, the Lord descended from heaven toward a multitude of them, and He came down and stood in their midst. As they pressed forward by His invitation to feel the prints of the nails in His hands and in His feet, He said, "I am the God of Israel, and the God of the whole earth, and have been slain for the sins of the world."[10]

189

Sun begins to break through the thick clouds of morning on the road to Damascus. Five or six days of travel would be required to take the 130-mile trip from Jerusalem to Damascus. Ananias, who lived on the street called Straight, was concerned about the Lord's sending Saul to him. "I have heard by many of this man, how much evil he hath done," he said. But the Lord replied, "He is a chosen vessel unto me."[11]

The resurrection of Jesus Christ did not end the persecution of His followers. If anything it was heightened as well-educated Pharisees like Saul of Tarsus breathed out "threatenings and slaughter against the disciples of the Lord"[12] and burst into houses, raising havoc and bringing men and women bound to prison. For those who would follow the Lord, the price was unspeakably dear. With Saul consenting, Stephen was stoned to death with these words as his last: "Lord Jesus, receive my spirit."[13] Then as Saul was on his way to Damascus, bearing letters authorizing persecution of the Christians, "suddenly there shined round about him a light from heaven: and he fell to the earth, and heard a voice saying unto him, Saul, Saul, why persecutest thou me? And he said, Who art thou, Lord? And the Lord said, I am Jesus whom thou persecutest."[14] Trembling and three days blind, Saul went to Damascus on a different errand—to be instructed in the gospel and then, converted and called Paul, to teach the word through all the Roman Empire.

Cornelius of Caesarea was a centurion of the Italian band, a devout man who, with all his house, feared God. An angel came to him in vision, telling him to send men to Joppa and ask for Peter at the seaside home of Simon the tanner. The next day, about noon, Peter was on the housetop praying when he became very hungry and would have eaten. While he prepared, he fell into a vision and saw a great sheet knit at four corners which was let down to the earth. In the sheet "were all manner of fourfooted beasts of the earth, and wild beasts, and creeping things, and fowls of the air. And there came a voice to him, Rise, Peter; kill, and eat." Could anything have been more repugnant to Peter than these things, all considered by the Jews to be common and unclean? But the message became clear: "What God hath cleansed, that call not thou common." Though it had been unlawful for a Jew to keep company with or to teach one of another nation, the message was sure: people like Cornelius must be taught. "I should not call any man common or unclean."[15]

Traditional site celebrated as the house of Simon the tanner in Joppa on the Mediterranean coast. Peter was praying about noon when he saw the great vision that taught him that the Lord desired to take the gospel message to all nations. As Peter was pondering what the vision meant, the men who were sent from Cornelius were standing at the gate of the home. The Spirit told Peter, "Go with them, doubting nothing: for I have sent them."[16]

Above: Theater at Caesarea on the Mediterranean Sea built by Herod the Great. Part of Paul's mission was to testify before kings, and this is where Paul testified before King Agrippa, saying, "Believest thou the prophets? I know that thou believest." To Agrippa's noncommittal response Paul exclaimed, "I would to God, that . . . all that hear me this day, were . . . such as I am."[17]

Right: Detail of Roman capital on ruins in city of Capernaum. Paul warned of the impending apostasy of the church: "I know this, that after my departing shall grievous wolves enter in among you, not sparing the flock. Also of your own selves shall men arise, speaking perverse things, to draw away disciples after them."[18] He further warned about these "having a form of godliness; but denying the power thereof: from such turn away."[19]

While a prisoner for preaching of Christ, Paul pleaded his case in Caesarea before King Agrippa, telling his history and claiming, I witness "none other things than those which the prophets and Moses did say should come. That Christ should suffer, . . . and that he should rise from the dead."[20] Callous Agrippa, who had been eager to hear Paul, said, "You think it will not take much . . . to make a Christian of me."[21] Paul, Peter, and the other apostles had no illusions that their efforts would be richly rewarded and that the kingdom of God would roll forth triumphant in their day.

When Christ had ascended into heaven, two men clothed in white had stood by the onlookers, saying, "Ye men of Galilee, why stand ye gazing up into heaven? this same Jesus, which is taken up from you into heaven, shall so come in like manner as ye have seen him go into heaven."[22] Yes, the Lord would come again, next time in triumph, but "that day shall not come, except there come a falling away first,"[23] wrote Paul to the Thessalonians. The apostles did not expect that the church they formed would survive their generation. Sometimes they were quite somber at the thought. "Never is there any mention of relief on the way, of happy times ahead, of final victory for the cause, or of the consoling thought that generations yet unborn will call one blessed."[24] Instead, as Paul writes "we are troubled on every side, yet not distressed; we are perplexed, but not in despair; persecuted, but not forsaken; cast down, but not destroyed."[25]

Their hope was not for today but for another world. Critics would make a heyday over Christ's failure to convert the world and His seeming inability to protect devotees from pain and persecution. To join the Church in that day was to be prepared to die. Yet it was exactly as He had said it would be. If the world had not accepted Him, it would not accept His disciples.

How would this falling away happen? "The apostasy described in the New Testament is not *desertion* of the cause, but *perversion* of it, a process by which 'the righteous are removed and none perceives it.'"[26] The vineyard is not attacked from without; it is seized by the husbandmen and the ancient church fades away.

O Jerusalem, . . . your house is left unto you desolate."[27] Christ had so prophesied, and so it would be. Who could have believed it amid the peace and prosperity Jerusalem enjoyed? Yet in A.D. 66, the mad Roman emperor Caligula attempted to have his image installed in the temple, and extremist groups stirred the nation to revolt. Titus led a long and bitter Roman siege upon the city, made worse because opposing Jewish factions fought each other, killing priests at the altar in the temple, leaving carcasses and pools of blood on the marble floor. The temple was burnt to ashes, its sacred relics carried off to Rome, and Titus, infuriated against the Jews, undertook the task of well-nigh exterminating them—crucifying them by the hundreds, selling them into slavery, starving them until they turned on each other. Josephus says that immediately after the siege, if a Jew had come upon the city suddenly, however well he had known it before, he would have asked, "What place is this?" Nothing remained of the beauty of Judea.

Left: Northwestern wall of settlement of Masada intact at the top of sheer cliffs with a Roman ramp visible in the background (a road cuts across it). As the city was about to fall to the brutal Roman forces, Eleazar, the leader of these Zealots, said, "Let us destroy our money and the fortress by fire; . . . and let us spare nothing but our provisions; for they will be a testimonial when we are dead that we were not subdued for want of necessaries; but that, according to our original resolution, we have preferred death before slavery."[28]

Above: Remains at Masada of the oldest synagogue in the world. Masada is in a remote region at the extreme south end of the Dead Sea. So that the Romans would not take away their freedom, the Zealots took their own lives. "Let our wives die before they are abused," Eleazar pleaded, "and our children before they have tasted of slavery, . . . and why are we afraid of death, while we are pleased with the rest that we have in sleep?"[29] Here 953 people were killed.

195

God's covenant people had been scattered, their nation destroyed by A.D. 73. They had missed their King when He had come. The ancient Christian church faced its own problems. As one by one the apostles were killed, by the end of the first century something was lost. Priesthood power was taken from the earth. Doctrines were transformed or invented, having no scriptural basis, until the light flickered out altogether. The early church fathers who followed Christ's apostles felt this loss. A lamenting touches much of their writing: "There will come a time when you will call upon me and I shall not hear you."[30] Other dispensations had ended with apostasy brought on by wickedness. This time it was no different. The heavens were closed, revelation had ceased for wickedness, and for generations a deep spiritual sleep fell upon the people. Many claimed to act for the Lord, even did atrocities in His name, but His teachings had been perverted. Salvation without works. No miracles, no signs, no prophets, no revelation. It was indeed a dark age.

Yet Jesus had promised that He would come again to the earth, this time to reign in glory. How could this happen without a "restitution of all things,"[31] the keys, knowledge, and spiritual gifts that had been part of the ancient church? The heavens must again be opened and spiritual knowledge be poured out upon the earth that a generation could be ready to meet Him when He came. Certainly many people over the centuries, longing for the light, had looked for such a day. So it was that on a spring morning in 1830 in Palmyra, New York, a boy named Joseph Smith walked into a grove of trees to pray. He had a serious question. Having investigated the sects of his day with their warring doctrines, he simply wanted to know for himself. Which church should he join? Then, suddenly, he said, "I saw two Personages, whose brightness and glory defy all description, standing above me in the air. One of them spake unto me, calling me by name and said, pointing to the other—*This is My Beloved Son. Hear Him!*"[32] The restoration had begun, and God established His Church once again upon the earth.[33]

Pages 196–97: Waves crash into a reef on the Mediterranean Sea coast about twenty miles to the south of Haifa. Those who use the Bible as a pattern to try to find the true church that Christ established will have to find one with twelve apostles and prophets; the priesthood offices of deacon, teacher, priest, elder, seventy, and high priest; spiritual gifts such as healings and speaking in tongues; the laying on of hands for the gift of the Holy Ghost; saving ordinances for the dead; and a mission to take the gospel to every nation, kindred, tongue, and people.

Above: Detail of olive-oil lamps burning brightly in the night on part of an ancient olive press near Bethlehem. The Lord gives modern revelation to interpret the parable of the ten virgins: "They that are wise and have received the truth, and have taken the Holy Spirit for their guide, and have not been deceived—verily I say unto you, they shall not be hewn down and cast into the fire, but shall abide the day."[34]

When will the Lord return? It is a question always on the minds of the faithful. When His apostles asked this as they sat together on the Mount of Olives the last week of His life, Jesus answered, "Now learn a parable of the fig tree; when his branch is yet tender, and putteth forth leaves, ye know that summer is nigh."[35] The signs are clear. So it would be with the Lord's second coming. Though He would not tell them the exact day or hour of His return, "in that day when they shall see all these things, then shall they know that the hour is nigh"[36]

For those whose eyes do not see signs and wonders, His return will come as a surprise. As it was in the days of Noah, when people were "eating and drinking, marrying and giving in marriage, . . . and knew not until the flood came, and took them all away," so will it be for the spiritually blind when the Lord comes again. It will be sudden, unexpected, like a thief in the night. In that day, "shall two be in the field; the one shall be taken, and the other left. Two women shall be grinding at the mill; the one shall be taken, and the other left."[37] Watch and pray therefore, the Lord advised, lest at anytime you are overtaken with the cares of life and the day come upon you unaware.

"The kingdom of heaven," said the Lord, "[shall] be likened unto ten virgins, which took their lamps, and went forth to meet the bridegroom." Hebrew wedding ceremonies were held in the evening, and it was the custom in the East to carry lamps filled with olive oil to light the way as they went out to join the bridal procession. In this parable, the Lord uses oil to represent spiritual preparation, something that cannot be borrowed at the last minute. Five foolish virgins took their lamps and brought no oil with them. "But the wise took oil in their vessels with their lamps." While they waited for the bridegroom, they slept. Then suddenly at midnight (a most surprising time, when one would least expect it) the bridegroom came. All the virgins arose to trim their lamps, but the foolish cried, "Give us of your oil; for our lamps are gone out." The wise answered, "Not so; . . . go ye rather to them that sell, and buy for yourselves. And while they went to buy, the bridegroom came; and they that were ready went in with him to the marriage: and the door was shut."[38]

Beautiful leaves of a fig tree bathed in light at Tel Dan in the north of Israel. "Ye look and behold the fig trees, and ye see them with your eyes, and ye say when they begin to shoot forth, and their leaves are yet tender, that summer is now nigh at hand."[39] The Lord taught this to his disciples so that they might know that when all the signs began to be manifest, His coming would be nigh at hand.

Before the Lord comes again, the powers of evil will be unleashed as never before. It will be a day when evil will be taken for good and good, evil, when people take darkness for light and light for darkness.[40] False systems of belief and religion will so cover the earth with power and pomp, with the sway of mass opinion, that even if possible the very elect may be deceived. In that day many will say, "Do this, or do that, and it mattereth not." They will deny the power of God, saying that miracles have ceased. They will harden their hearts and oppress their neighbors.

It will be a time of "wars and rumors of wars, and the whole earth shall be in commotion, . . . and the love of men shall wax cold."[41] "And there shall be earthquakes also in divers places, and many desolations; yet men will harden their hearts against me." "And they shall see signs and wonders. . . . And they shall behold blood, and fire, and vapors of smoke. And before the day of the Lord shall come, the sun shall be darkened, and the moon be turned into blood, and the stars fall from heaven." A desolating scourge shall cover the land. Amid this misery, hounded on every side by war, famine, and pestilence, "men's hearts shall fail them, and they shall say that Christ delayeth his coming." Still the Lord gives this comfort: "Be not troubled, for, when all these things shall come to pass, ye may know that the promises which have been made unto you shall be fulfilled."[42] He will come to put an end to all pain.

Yet before He comes, the gospel must be preached to all the earth, and the dispersed and scattered remnants of Israel will be gathered together. The lost ten tribes will return, bringing their records, and Zion will be built. Then in the final scenes, Israel will be under siege by an army of two hundred million with destructive weapons as have never before been seen. The focus of the worldwide conflict will be the valley of Armageddon. Jerusalem will be taken and pillaged, her women ravished. When the battle seems all but lost, with the two prophets who have been defending Jerusalem for three and a half years lying dead in the street—then the great God, Jesus Christ, will put His foot on the Mount of Olives and save His covenant people.

Pages 200–201: Standing on the edge of the hills of Nazareth looking southwest into the Jezreel Valley. The Lord talks of the cry of the rich in the last days, those who have not given of their substance to the poor: "Your riches will canker your souls; and this shall be your lamentation in the day of visitation, and of judgment, and of indignation: The harvest is past, the summer is ended, and my soul is not saved!"[43]

Above: Rare heavy moisture in early morning fills valleys around the hills of Jerusalem. When the Lord comes, He "shall be red in his apparel, and his garments like him that treadeth in the wine-vat. . . . And his voice shall be heard: I have trodden the wine-press alone."[44] *The prophecies are "that unto me every knee shall bow, every tongue shall swear"*[45] *that "Jesus Christ is Lord, to the glory of God the Father."*[46]

To speak of the Lord's second coming is to speak of many appearances, some private, some public. At Adam-ondi-Ahman, in western Missouri, He will come to an assembly of faithful Saints, joined together from every dispensation. There they will return their keys and give an accounting of their stewardships. He will appear with 144,000 high priests on Mt. Zion. He will come quietly to the temples in Jerusalem and in Zion. At that critical moment during the final war of Armageddon when Jerusalem is overrun, He will set foot on the Mount of Olives, and the earth will split open with a thunderous, roaring earthquake, sending upheavals worldwide. This will be part of the tumult that causes every valley to be exalted and every mountain to be made low. Then, at long last, many of the Jews will recognize Him. "And they shall look upon [him] whom they have pierced." "And one shall say unto him, What are these wounds in thine hands?" He shall answer, "Those with which I was wounded in the house of my friends."[47]

Then, "let the floods clap their hands; let the hills be joyful."[48] That day will arrive when Jesus, who once came as a fragile infant, will return as the glorified king before all the people of the earth. "For as the light of the morning cometh out of the east, and shineth even unto the west, and covereth the whole earth, so shall also the coming of the Son of Man be."[49]

Angelic trumpets will herald the word, choirs will sing in praise and adoration, and, with a host of resurrected Saints, Christ will return in clouds of glory and devouring fire. The burnings will melt the mountains like wax, melt the very elements of the earth, and the wicked will be scorched as stubble.

This will be the end of the world, that oppressive, exploiting, abusing world, but not the end of the earth. The righteous, with the yoke of the world removed from their shoulders, will be caught up to meet the One who had always borne their afflictions. Of those it is said, "Thine eyes shall see the king in his beauty."[50] Their millennial inheritance is the joy of a new heaven and a new earth.

Pages 204–5: View of the lush, beautiful earth, looking from the top of Mt. Tabor toward a portion of the Jezreel Valley. The earth longs to be freed from the sins and stains of man, to bring forth in all her abundance and glory. Truly we shall sing with renewed meaning in the day of the Lord Jesus, "How blessed the day when the lamb and the lion Shall lie down together without any ire, And Ephraim be crowned with his blessing in Zion, As Jesus descends with his chariot of fire! We'll sing and we'll shout with the armies of heaven, Hosanna, hosanna to God and the Lamb! Let glory to them in the highest be given, Henceforth and forever, Amen and amen!"[51]

The heavens have smiled upon [the earth]; and she is clothed with the glory of her God; for he stands in the midst of his people."[52] In that millennial day for which we yearn, Jesus Christ, who once walked the earth blessing with a word or a touch, then will dwell with the righteous for a thousand years. Gone will be scarcity, the fear that haunts our sleep, the loneliness that makes us feel like strangers here. Forgotten will be enmity, the pride that drives us to best a brother, the anger that turns to violence and war. Only the dimmest memory will be disease, death, tears shed for the long absence of a loved one. All that has been pain, grief, and disappointment will be swallowed up in His loving presence. "He is come!" we will shout in glad hosannas. "He is come."

The Lord's second coming will herald the morning of the first resurrection when the just shall arise from their graves. The little graves of children, the forgotten tombs of generations past—these will burst open and give forth their dead. "Awake and sing, ye that dwell in the dust."[53] Amid new harmonies loved ones will fall on each others' necks in unspeakable joy. In that day, "the spirit and the body shall be reunited again in its perfect form," each "raised to happiness according to his desires of happiness."[54]

Released from oppression, the earth will be as Eden, giving bounteously. Then will begin the thousand years of peace that all the faithful have prayed for when they have said, "Thy kingdom come."[55] Worldly political regimes with their ambitions and intrigues will have been toppled, and Christ will reign personally upon the earth. Satan will be bound by the righteousness of the people, and they will not "learn war any more."[56] The mighty military arsenals that have sapped the wealth of nations will be beaten into plowshares.[57] The Lord said, "I am come that they might have life, and that they might have it more abundantly."[58] Then will be the time of abundance in spirit, joy, love, and knowledge such as we who dwell in a fallen world can scarcely comprehend. The Lord who once came to us as the babe in Bethlehem is the author of it all. This is "written, that ye might believe that Jesus is the Christ, the Son of God; and that believing ye might have life through his name."[59]

NOTES

PERSONAL NOTES

1. 2 Kings 6:16, 17.
2. Isaiah 35:1.
3. 2 Nephi 25:23.
4. John 21:5.

SECTION 1:

I AM HE WHO WAS PREPARED FROM THE FOUNDATION OF THE WORLD

1. John 1:1, 14.
2. John 17:5.
3. Exodus 33:11.
4. William Wordsworth, "Ode on Intimations of Immortality," as quoted in LeGrand Richards, *A Marvelous Work and a Wonder* (Salt Lake City: Deseret Book Co., 1950), p. 301.
5. Joseph Smith, *History of The Church of Jesus Christ of Latter-day Saints*, 7 vols. (Salt Lake City: Deseret Book Co., 1980), 5:337. Hereinafter referred to as HC.
6. D&C 93:33.
7. HC 6:308.
8. See Job 38:7.
9. Abraham 3:24–25.
10. See 1 Nephi 15:34; Alma 40:26, Ephesians 5:5.
11. Alma 13:12.
12. Alma 34:10.
13. Moses 4:2.
14. Mosiah 3:17; see also Acts 4:12.
15. D&C 45:5.
16. See Isaiah 14:12.
17. Moses 4:1.
18. Isaiah 14:13, 14.
19. Moses 4:3.
20. Revelation 12:7–9.
21. Jeremiah 1:5.
22. Joseph Fielding Smith, *Doctrines of Salvation*, compiled by Bruce R. McConkie (Salt Lake City: Bookcraft, 1986), 1:90.
23. D&C 138:39.
24. D&C 138:37.
25. D&C 138:38.
26. Abraham 3:22, 23.
27. Alma 13:3, 6.
28. See Romans 8:25.
29. 1 Peter 1:7.
30. Numbers 20:11.
31. D&C 1:38.
32. John 1:3.

33. D&C 104:17.
34. Job 38:4, 5.
35. D&C 88:7–10.
36. Moses 6:63.
37. See Genesis 1:14.
38. Moses 1:39.
39. *Hymns of The Church of Jesus Christ of Latter-day Saints* (Salt Lake City: Deseret Book Co., 1985), no. 62. Hereinafter referred to as *Hymns*.
40. *Smith's Bible Dictionary* (Grand Rapids, Mich.: Zondervan Publishing House, 1976), p. 31.
41. Moses 6:63.
42. Genesis 2:16–17.
43. Genesis 2:23.
44. Jolene Edmunds Rockwood, "The Redemption of Eve," in *Sisters in Spirit*, ed. Maureen Ursenbach Beecher and Lavina Fielding Anderson (Chicago: University of Illinois Press, 1987), p. 18.
45. Moses 2:28.
46. Moses 4:6, 10–11.
47. Moses 4:23, 25.
48. Moses 5:11.
49. Moses 5:7.
50. Mosiah 3:13.
51. Moses 5:9.
52. Moses 7:4.
53. Joseph Smith Translation, Genesis 14:30–31. Hereinafter Joseph Smith Translation is referred to as JST.
54. Moses 7:13.
55. Genesis 22:3.
56. Abraham 2:8, 10–11.
57. Romans 4:20–21.
58. Genesis 22:2.
59. See Hugh Nibley, *Nibley on the Timely and the Timeless* (Provo, Ut.: BYU Religious Studies Center, 1978), p. 134.
60. Genesis 22:11–12.
61. Abraham 2:7.
62. Romans 8:28.
63. Genesis 39:2–3; 41:33, 38.
64. Genesis 42:2.
65. See Genesis 37:24–25.
66. Exodus 3:5, 7.
67. Exodus 3:13–14.
68. Moses 1:2, 9–10.
69. JST Matthew 9:18–19.

70. 2 Nephi 11:4.
71. JST Exodus 34:1–2.
72. Galatians 3:24.
73. Jacob 4:5.
74. 1 Nephi 17:41.
75. Deuteronomy 8:2–3.
76. *Eusebius' Ecclesiastical History* (Grand Rapids, Mich.: Baker Book House, 1976), p. 22.
77. Jacob 4:4.
78. 1 Nephi 13:24, 26.
79. Isaiah 7:14.
80. 2 Nephi 9:8, 20.
81. 1 Nephi 11:31.
82. Psalm 22:1, 7–8, 16, 18.
83. Isaiah 9:6.
84. See Numbers 24:17.
85. Isaiah 47:4.
86. 1 Kings 18:37–38, 45.
87. Isaiah 5:1–2.
88. Jacob 5:7.
89. 3 Nephi 17:4.
90. Psalm 137:1.
91. Alfred Edersheim, *The Life and Times of Jesus the Messiah* (Iowa Falls, Iowa: World Bible Publishers, 1971), 1:132.

SECTION 2:

BEHOLD THE LAMB OF GOD

1. Luke 1:17, 20, 62.
2. Matthew 3:3.
3. Genesis 30:1.
4. Luke 1:30, 34–35, 38, 43.
5. Luke 1:46–47.
6. Matthew 1:19, 20.
7. Luke 2:7.
8. JST Luke 2:7.
9. Matthew 8:20.
10. Luke 2:6.
11. Alma 7:10.
12. Luke 2:7.
13. See *Lost Books of the Bible* (New York: Alpha House, 1926), pp. 18–19.
14. See D&C 20:1.
15. Luke 2:9.
16. JST Luke 2:10–14.
17. Luke 2:15.
18. Matthew 2:2.
19. JST Matthew 3:6.
20. Matthew 2:8.
21. 1 Samuel 13:14.
22. See Genesis 49:24.
23. Luke 2:26, 29.
24. JST Luke 2:35.

25. Frederic W. Farrar, *The Life of Christ* (Portland: Fountain Publications, 1964), p. 61.
26. Matthew 2:18.
27. From "The Protevangelion of James," in *The Lost Books of the Bible* (New York: Alpha House, 1926), pp. 35–36.
28. Exodus 4:22.
29. Matthew 2:15.
30. James E. Talmage, *Jesus the Christ* (Salt Lake City: Deseret Book Co., 1982), p. 101.
31. D. Kelly Ogden, *Where Jesus Walked* (Salt Lake City: Deseret Book Co., 1991), p. 152.
32. Matthew 21:13; see also Ogden, *Where Jesus Walked*, p. 153.
33. JST Luke 2:46.
34. Luke 6:3.
35. JST Luke 2:48–49.
36. Ogden, *Where Jesus Walked*, p. 98.
37. Matthew 7:24.
38. Luke 14:28.
39. See Edersheim, *Jesus the Messiah*, 1:228; D&C 88:119–20.
40. Psalm 121:8.
41. Luke 2:52, 40.
42. See D&C 93: 12–13.
43. JST Matthew 3:25.
44. Edersheim, *Jesus the Messiah*, 1:223.
45. John 1:46.
46. Luke 2:19.
47. Talmage, *Jesus the Christ*, p. 109.
48. JST Matthew 3:26.
49. Matthew 3:2, 4.
50. D&C 84:28.
51. Luke 3:11.
52. Luke 3:7–8, 23.
53. HC 5:260–61.
54. See Joshua 3:14–17.
55. Edersheim, *Jesus the Messiah*, 2:746.
56. Moses 6:64–65.
57. JST Matthew 3:42–43.
58. 2 Nephi 31:5.
59. JST Matthew 3:44–46.
60. JST Genesis 17:11.
61. JST John 1:20–21, 22, 24.
62. JST Luke 3:5, 7.
63. Matthew 3:11.
64. JST John 1:31–32.

25. Frederic W. Farrar,
65. John 3:30.
66. John 5:35.
67. Edersheim, *Jesus the Messiah*, 1:277.
68. See *Josephus*, trans. William Whiston (Grand Rapids, Mich.: Kregel Publications, 1974), p. 343.
69. JST Matthew 4:1.
70. Luke 6:12.
71. 3 Nephi 17:16.
72. See D&C 59:14.
73. Isaiah 58:6.
74. Matthew 4:3.
75. Matthew 4:4, 6, 7.
90. D&C 50:41.
76. See D. Kelly Ogden and Jeffrey R. Chadwick, *The Holy Land* (Jerusalem: HaMakor, 1990), pp. 227–28.
78. Matthew 7:29.
79. Isaiah 2:3.
80. John 1:36, 39.
81. John 1:41, 43, 45, 46.
82. John 1:47–48.
83. Mosiah 8:17.
84. John 1:49–50.
85. John 10:14.
86. Matthew 10:29–30.
87. Edersheim, *Jesus the Messiah*, 1:353.
88. John 2:4.
89. JST John 2:4.
90. John 2:8.
91. John 2:10.
92. John 10:10.
93. 2 Baruch 29:5.
94. Talmage, *Jesus the Christ*, p. 137.
95. *Smith's Bible Dictionary*, p. 589.
96. See Numbers 11:16, 17.
97. John 3:2.
98. Edersheim, *Jesus the Messiah*, 1:381.
99. John 3:3.
100. Mosiah 5:2, 7.
101. Galatians 5:22.
102. John 3:8.
103. John 4:29.
104. Talmage, *Jesus the Christ*, p. 59.
105. John 4:7, 10.
106. D&C 14:7.
107. John 4:19.
108. JST John 4:28.
109. Luke 4:16.
110. Edersheim, *Jesus the Messiah*, 1:439, 440.
111. Luke 4:18–19. See also Isaiah 61:1–2.

112. Luke 4:20–21.
113. Mark 6:3.
114. Luke 4:28–30.
115. Mark 6:3.
116. Luke 5:6.
117. See Edersheim, *Jesus the Messiah*, 1:475.
118. JST Matthew 4:18.
119. See Edersheim, *Jesus the Messiah*, 1:474.
120. JST Matthew 4:19, 20.
121. John 6:67–69.
122. Luke 4:37.
123. Matthew 4:24.
124. Isaiah 61:3.
125. Mark 1:33.
126. Luke 4:40.
127. Mark 1:37.
128. Isaiah 49:13.
129. Matthew 9:2.
130. Luke 5:21.
131. Matthew 9:5.
132. Luke 5:26.
133. *Smith's Bible Dictionary*, p. 508.
134. Isaiah 11:2.
135. John 5:19; Luke 6:9.
136. Matthew 12:8.
137. John 5:3.
138. Ephesians 2:20.
139. Luke 6:12.
140. John 15:16.
141. 1 Corinthians 1:26–27.
142. JST Matthew 10:14, 19.
143. Matthew 10:8, 19.
144. Matthew 10:40.
145. D&C 84:38.
146. JST Ephesians 4:13–14.
147. See Revelation 21:14.

SECTION 3:

THAT THEY MIGHT HAVE LIFE MORE ABUNDANTLY

1. JST Matthew 5:15, 16.
2. Matthew 5:4.
3. *Prayers of the Cosmos*, trans. Neil Douglas-Klotz (San Francisco: Harper & Row, 1990), p. 50.
4. Matthew 5:5.
5. Douglas-Klotz, *Prayers of the Cosmos*, p. 53.
6. Matthew 5:8.
7. Douglas-Klotz, *Prayers of the Cosmos*, p. 62.

8. Matthew 5:7.

9. Douglas-Klotz, *Prayers of the Cosmos*, p. 59.

10. Matthew 6:20, 19.

11. 3 Nephi 9:19–20.

12. Alma 22:18.

13. D&C 67:10.

14. Luke 18:1–14.

15. Matthew 6:6.

16. Matthew 5:23–24, 39, 44.

17. Matthew 5:48.

18. Matthew 6:24, 22.

19. JST Matthew 6:32–34.

20. JST Matthew 6:28.

21. Catherine Thomas, "The Sermon on the Mount," in *Studies in Scripture, The Gospels* ed. Kent P. Jackson and Robert L. Millet (Salt Lake City: Deseret Book Co., 1986), p. 245.

22. Matthew 6:27.

23. Matthew 6:8.

24. See John 15:5.

25. Alma 37:36.

26. Matthew 7:7.

27. JST Matthew 7:17–20.

28. *Hymns*, no. 221.

29. Luke 7:13, 14, 15.

30. Luke 7:38, 39, 44–47.

31. Mark 2:16–17.

32. Matthew 13:3–9.

33. Edersheim, *Jesus the Messiah*, 1:586–87.

34. Matthew 13:10, 11, 19–23.

35. D&C 82:3.

36. Matthew 13:24–25, 28.

37. See *Smith's Bible Dictionary*, p. 674.

38. D&C 86:2–3, 4, 6–7.

39. See *Smith's Bible Dictionary*, p. 674.

40. D&C 86:7; see also JST Matthew 13:29.

41. Matthew 13:44.

42. Talmage, *Jesus the Christ*, p. 273.

43. Mark 7:31.

44. Matthew 9:35.

45. Bruce R. McConkie, *The Mortal Messiah* (Salt Lake City: Deseret Book Co., 1980), 2:304.

46. Matthew 9:37.

47. John 3:26.

48. Matthew 11:3, 7.

49. JST Matthew 4:11.

50. Mark 6:20, 22.

51. McConkie, *Mortal Messiah*, 2:369.

52. Mark 6:31, 34.

53. Mark 6:35, 37; John 6:9; Mark 6:41–42.

54. John 6:15.

55. Matthew 17:27.

56. Matthew 14:22.

57. John 19:15.

58. Mark 6:48, 49.

59. Luke 8:23.

60. Mark 4:38–41.

61. John 6:20.

62. Matthew 14:28–29, 30–31.

63. John 6:20.

64. JST John 6:26.

65. New Revised Standard Version, John 6:27. Hereinafter referred to as NRSV.

66. JST John 6:27.

67. John 6:28–29, 31, 30.

68. NRSV, John 6:32.

69. John 6:34–35.

70. John 6:66.

71. Matthew 23:14.

72. Luke 11:43.

73. Matthew 23:14, 27.

74. Mark 7:5.

75. Mark 12:14.

76. JST Matthew 7:33.

77. Luke 8:40.

78. Mark 5:23.

79. Luke 8:43–44, 49.

80. Mark 5:30.

81. Luke 8:45, 47, 48.

82. Mark 5:35.

83. Luke 8:50.

84. Mark 5:38, 39–40, 41.

85. Matthew 8:28.

86. Mark 5:3, 7.

87. James 2:19.

88. Mark 5:9.

89. Mark 9:24.

90. Mark 5:19, 20.

91. Luke 18:1.

92. James 1:6.

93. Luke 18:2, 4, 5.

94. Luke 15:11–12.

95. Kenneth W. Godfrey, "The Surprise Factors in the Teachings of Jesus," in *The Lord of the Gospels* (Salt Lake City: Deseret Book Co., 1991), pp. 58, 59.

96. Luke 15:17–19.

97. Kenneth Bailey as quoted in Godfrey, "The Surprise Factors in the Teachings of Jesus," p. 59.

98. Luke 15:20, 31–32.

99. See Matthew 18:23–35. One talent of gold weighs 75.6 lbs.

100. Matthew 18:1.

101. Luke 22:24.

102. C. S. Lewis, *Mere Christianity* (New York: Macmillan, 1960), p. 95.

103. Matthew 18:4.

104. Mosiah 3:19.

105. Matthew 25:34, 35–40.

106. D&C 38:24, 26.

107. Matthew 16:13; see also Mark 8:27.

108. Matthew 16:15–17.

109. Matthew 16:18.

110. Matthew 17:1, 2.

111. Matthew 17:2.

112. JST Luke 9:29.

113. Mark 9:3.

114. Luke 9:22.

115. Matthew 16:22.

116. Matthew 16:19.

117. Matthew 17:5.

118. D&C 63:21.

119. Matthew 18:21, 22.

120. D&C 64:10.

121. John 7: 40–41, 16.

122. John 8:4–5.

123. John 8:6, 7.

124. John 8:9–11.

125. JST John 8:11.

126. D&C 58:42.

127. D&C 58:43.

128. John 8:39, 37, 56, 58.

129. Exodus 3:14.

130. D&C 132:37.

131. John 9:2, 3.

132. John 9:15, 22.

133. Edersheim, *Jesus the Messiah*, 2:184.

134. John 9:33, 38.

135. Edersheim, *Jesus the Messiah*, 2:178.

136. JST John 9:32.

137. Mosiah 3:13, circa 124 B.C.

138. John R. Lasater, "Shepherds of Israel," *Ensign*, May 1988, p. 74.

139. John 10:14, 27.

140. Psalm 23.

141. Mark 10:14.

142. See 3 Nephi 17:11–24.

143. Matthew 18:6.

144. Mark 10:17.

145. Matthew 19:17, 20, 21, 22.

146. Alma 34:28.

147. Matthew 19:26.

148. Luke 11:1, 2–4.

149. Douglas-Klotz, *Prayers of the Cosmos*, p. 12.

150. JST Luke 11:4.

151. Douglas-Klotz, *Prayers of the Cosmos*, p. 30.

152. JST Matthew 6:14.

153. Douglas-Klotz, *Prayers of the Cosmos*, p. 34.

154. Matthew 6:13.

155. Luke 10:40–42.

156. Luke 10:27, 29, 31.

157. Godfrey, "The Surprise Factors in the Teachings of Jesus," p. 63.

158. Luke 10:33–35, 37.

159. John 11:34, 39.

160. John 11:3, 4.

161. John 11:7, 16; JST v. 16.

162. John 11:21, 22.

163. John 11:23–27.

164. John 11:28, 34–35.

165. John 11:39, 41, 43–44, 53.

166. John 11:47.

SECTION 4:
MINE HOUR HAS COME

1. John 11:48.

2. John 12:27.

3. John 12:7.

4. John 12:49–50.

5. John 17:21.

6. John 12:44.

7. Luke 19:38.

8. Mark 11:2–3.

9. From the song "Jerusalem of Gold," by Shemer.

10. Edersheim, *Jesus the Messiah*, 2:369.

11. Luke 23: 29–30.

12. Matthew 7:20.

13. Luke 19:46.

14. Luke 20:2.

15. Luke 20:9.

16. Mark 12:1, 3, 6.

17. Jacob 5:41.

18. Isaiah 5:2.

19. Mark 12:9.

20. Mark 11:30–33.

21. Luke 22:3.

22. Matthew 27:3–8.

23. 1 Nephi 11:33.

24. John 13:33, 2, 4.

25. John 13:8–9, 14.

26. Mark 14:18–19.

27. John 13:26.

28. Matthew 26:25.

29. John 13:27.

30. John 13:33, 34.

31. JST Matthew 26:22–24.

32. Mark 14:27, 29.

33. Luke 22:33–34.

34. John 14:27.

35. John 14:18, 17.

36. John 14:5, 6, 2.

37. John 15:5.

38. Talmage, *Jesus the Christ*, p. 561.

39. John 15:7.

40. John 16:23.

41. John 16:27.

42. See John 15:9.

43. John 15:13.

44. John 16:20–21.

45. John 16:2–3, 4.

46. John 17:9, 15.

47. Mark 14:33.

48. Matthew 26:38, 39.

49. Luke 22:42.

50. Mark 14:36.

51. Talmage, *Jesus the Christ*, pp. 568–69.

52. D&C 19:16–18.

53. James 5:14.

54. John 3:16.

55. Luke 22:43–44.

56. John 14:9.

57. See D&C 130:7.

58. 2 Nephi 9:14.

59. Alma 36:18.

60. Orson F. Whitney, *Through Memory's Halls* (Independence, Mo.: Zion's Printing and Publishing Co., 1930), pp. 82–83.

61. *Hymns*, no. 193.

62. John 1:5.

63. Luke 22:45.

64. Matthew 26:40–41.

65. Mark 14:41.

66. Psalm 41:9.

67. Edersheim, *Jesus the Messiah*, 2:543.

68. Matthew 26:53.

69. Farrar, *Life of Christ*, p. 586.

70. McConkie, *The Mortal Messiah*, 4:150.

71. Farrar, *Life of Christ*, p. 597.

72. Matthew 26:62–63, 64.

73. John 18:17.

74. Matthew 26:71–72.

75. Mark 14:70.

76. John 18:26.

77. Luke 22:60.

78. Psalm 22:7.

79. Luke 22:64, 71.

80. John 18:29, 38.

81. Isaiah 53:3.

82. Luke 23:14.

83. Matthew 27:17.

84. Matthew 27:19.

85. John 19:3.

86. John 19:5, 4, 15.

87. Matthew 27:24–25.

88. *Hymns*, no. 86.

89. Farrar, *Life of Christ*, p. 619.

90. John 19:19.

91. Luke 23:34, 35; Matthew 27:43.

92. John 19:27.

93. Matthew 27:46; Mark 15:34.

94. JST Matthew 27:54.

95. Mark 15:39.

96. As quoted in Hugh Nibley, *Mormonism and Early Christianity* (Salt Lake City: Deseret Book Co., 1987), p. 116.

97. Ibid., p. 103.

98. D&C 138:12, 15, 18–19, 23–24.

99. Matthew 27:52.

100. D&C 138:29, 30.

101. 1 Corinthians 15:29.

102. John 20:2, 9, 8.

103. Luke 24:4–5.

104. JST Matthew 28:4–5.

105. Matthew 27:3–4.

106. *Hymns*, no. 136.

107. John 20:15, 16.

108. 1 Corinthians 15:20, 22.

109. JST John 20:17.

110. Luke 24:11.

111. *Hymns*, no. 199.

112. 1 Corinthians 15:55.

113. 2 Nephi 9:50.

114. Luke 24:16, 18, 19–20, 26, 27, 29, 30, 31, 32.

115. Luke 24:36, 39–41.

116. *Hymns*, no. 29.

SECTION 5:
THEN SHALL THEY KNOW THAT I AM THE LORD

1. Luke 22:31–32.

2. John 21:3, 5, 6, 7.

3. John 21:12, 15–17.

4. 1 Corinthians 15:6.

5. John 20:30.

6. See Nibley, *Mormonism and Early Christianity*, pp. 10–22.

7. Matthew 28:19.

8. Acts 1:8.

9. John 10:16.

10. 3 Nephi 11:14.

11. Acts 9:13, 15.

12. Acts 9:1.

13. Acts 7:59.

14. Acts 9:3–5.

15. Acts 10:12,13, 15, 28.

16. Acts 10:20.

17. Acts 26:27, 29.

18. Acts 20:29–30.

19. 2 Timothy 3:5.

20. Acts 26: 22, 23.

21. New English Bible, Acts 26:28.

22. Acts 1:11.

23. 2 Thessalonians 2:3.

24. Nibley, *Mormonism and Early Christianity*, p. 171.

25. 2 Corinthians 4:8–9.

26. Nibley, *Mormonism and Early Christianity*, p. 172.

27. Matthew 23:38.

28. Josephus, p. 601.

29. Ibid.

30. In Nibley, *Mormonism and Early Christianity*, p. 173.

31. Acts 3:21.

32. Joseph Smith–History 1:17.

33. See Scot Facer Proctor, *Witness of the Light* (Salt Lake City: Deseret Book Co., 1991).

34. D&C 45:57.

35. Matthew 24:32.

36. D&C 45:38.

37. Matthew 24:38–39, 40–41.

38. Matthew 25:1, 4, 8–10, 13.

39. D&C 45:37.

40. See Isaiah 5:20.

41. Mormon 8:31, 36.

42. D&C 45:26, 27, 33, 40–42, 26, 35.

43. D&C 56:16.

44. D&C 133:48, 50.

45. Isaiah 45:23.

46. Philippians 2:11–12.

47. Zechariah 12:10; 13:6.

48. Psalm 98:8.

49. Joseph Smith–Matthew 1:26.

50. Isaiah 33:17.

51. *Hymns*, no. 2.

52. D&C 84:101.

53. Isaiah 26:19.

54. Alma 11:43; 41:5.

55. Matthew 6:10.

56. Isaiah 2:4.

57. See Micah 4:3.

58. John 10:10.

59. John 20:31.

"Now I am no more in the world. . . .

Keep through thine own name those whom thou hast given me,

that they may be one, as we are."

(John 17:11.)

"And this is life eternal,

that they might know thee the only true God,

and Jesus Christ,

whom thou hast sent."

(John 17:3.)